The Inheritance

J.W. SCOTT

The Inheritance

ISBN: 978-1-943842-56-8

This book is dedicated to:

My wife, Lynn, my son, Kyle
and my daughter, Kristen.

around them. Too many memories. Bill was becoming more of a loner as the days passed. After the bank foreclosed on the house, he couldn't even afford to rent a small apartment, having used up most of his savings trying to locate Amber, hoping she was still alive, but knowing in his heart she wasn't.

Bill had to live somewhere and the rented ten-foot by thirty-foot storage bay for his tools and motorcycles looked like the best option, so he moved in after making a few changes for comfort. A refrigerator, TV and stereo made things a little better. No running water was an inconvenience, so showering at the truck stop was becoming a habit. There was a five-gallon plastic bucket with a lid for late night piss emergencies—a "slop bucket" as the old timers called it. Bill even rigged up an old toilet seat so it would be comfortable if the need arose. All in all, the place was habitable but still not a home. At least he was saving some money.

Bill worked all he could and tried to save everything he earned. He really wanted to buy a house, but his credit wasn't stellar. The only thing he knew to do was press on and hope for the best. Little did he realize that tonight his life would change beyond anything imaginable.

2

About the same time Bill was showering at the truck stop, a Wells Fargo armored truck was lumbering up Highway 64 towards Brevard. The truck had made the last stop in Hendersonville and as the driver backed out of the parking space his partner unexpectedly pulled his weapon and instructed him where to drive. The thought of all that money was just too much for the poor man—he wanted it all to himself.

At first, the driver assumed it was a joke, but when the barrel of the pistol poked between his ribs, he did as he was told.

"You know that we are being tracked by GPS," Robert, the driver, told his partner. "Put that thing away and I'll forget you ever had the notion. Hell,

I've even thought about doing the same thing on some days."

"Too late," was all Dave said.

The GPS had already been disabled. Dave wasn't the kind of man who could kill someone, but Robert didn't know that. They drove west on Highway 64 until Dave forced Robert to turn left onto Highway 191 toward Mills River.

A few miles down the road, Dave instructed Robert to turn right into a supermarket parking lot. With the pistol still stuck in his ribs, Robert protested, "Dave, regardless of how much money is back there, you're not going to get away with this. They will find you; they always do. Think about prison. Just think about all this."

Robert could feel the panic creeping in on him. He was no hero and there was no way he was going to get shot for someone else's money, so he shut up.

Dave looked into Robert's eyes and could see the fear. He grinned at Robert to ease the tension and said, "I am thinking, mostly about how much money is back there and the risk is worth it. There's nothing you can say that'll change my mind. From here on out keep your mouth shut, don't do anything stupid and we'll both be able to grow old." Dave looked around the parking lot. "There, next to that white pickup. Park there."

Robert did as he was told. It was then that Robert realized how serious the situation was becoming. As a short, balding man came to the driver's door, Robert began to tremble as Dave told him to open the door and get out.

"Remember, just do as you're told. No talking and everything will be ok. One more thing, these boys aren't as friendly as me," Dave told Robert as he nudged him out the door.

The short fellow grabbed Robert by the arm and escorted him to the pickup truck. Dave slid over into the driver's seat of the armored truck and drove away.

A hiker and his dog found Robert in his underwear, strapped to a tree in the Bent Creek area two days later. Cold and hungry, he couldn't give the FBI any useful information about the robbery. The truck had disappeared.

3

Bill got out of his truck as the mist turned to a light
rain. He unlocked the gate to the fence surround-
ing the five rows of storage buildings. All renters had
24-hour access to their storage cubicles.

Bill's bay was on the far side of the small complex.
He checked the office to make sure Steve, the owner,
wasn't there. He did this every night to ensure that he
wouldn't be caught—the lease agreement stated there
was not to be any "habitation." Bill could be evicted
if he was found to be living in the storage unit, then
what? He tried not thinking about things like that.
Walking between the fence and the last row of buildings, Bill came to #313, unlocking then raising the
roll-up door. He switched on the lights and surveyed
his domain. Two motorcycles were in the center floor

with a fridge and toolbox to the left. He had stacked small cardboard boxes up to form a wall at the back. This wall kept his bed and TV from being observed by anyone who might peek in when the door was up. It was depressing and with the sound of the door coming down he realized how alone he was. At least with the door closed he felt some security.

Weeks ago, Bill had figured out a system with the lock on the roll-up door. To anyone passing by it looked as if the padlock was locked and the bolt in place, but the only time it was really locked was when Bill wasn't there. He had also worked out the problem of raising the door and not being surprised by someone, especially the owner, by drilling a one-inch hole in the door at eye level. Poking a small mirror on a telescoping rod through the hole, he could see up and down the alley-way. When not in use, a small plug was inserted into the hole. The important thing was to keep everybody from knowing that someone was living in the space.

Bill bought water and stock piled it in several one gallon jugs. He tried to eat and cook with everything he used being disposable. There was one outlet in the warehouse. The refrigerator stayed plugged in all the time and he would have to switch out cords when something else needed to be powered. Once he was done cooking with the microwave, he would have to unplug it to listen to music or watch TV. The reason for this inconvenience was because several pods shared the same circuit. If a breaker tripped it would call attention to the situation. It was just one of many problems Bill worked out to stay invisible.

Behind the boxes was the "bedroom." Bill had laid down an area rug and hung an Indian print cloth on the back door. So much for interior design. Most of the rentals were 20 feet long with another 10 foot unit behind them. Bill, with permission, had removed the dividing partition to make his warehouse 30 feet long with a door at both ends. A chest of drawers, a wardrobe and a chair surrounded the bed. Things were tight, but clean and comfortable.

Pulling open the refrigerator door, Bill got out a gallon of water and made himself some pasta. It was already past 7:00 pm and he could feel the loneliness setting in deeper. Watching the water heat in the microwave he could see a faint reflection of himself in the glass. Staring into it, not being able to pull himself away, his mind searching for answers, he knew he had to break out of this funk. *But how?* he thought. He had saved up some money, but not enough to buy a house or land. Most of his so-called friends had abandoned him. Work was work and it sucked. His girlfriend was dead. And on top of that he lived in a warehouse where he had to piss in a bucket.

Bill usually comforted himself by saying, "It could be worse; it could be raining." But it didn't help tonight.

Shit, it is raining, he thought. *Well, it could be worse; I could be living under a bridge and it could be raining.* The bell on the microwave went off and startled him back to reality.

After eating, Bill sat on the bed. Now the reflection from the TV was staring back at him.

"What do you want?" he asked the reflection. "I just saw your twin in the microwave."

Man, he thought. *I've got to get out more. I'm talking to my reflections. This can't be good.*

Hitting the power button, both the TV and the DVD came on. *Maybe I can finish watching this movie. It's due back tomorrow.* With the TV turned down so low as to be barely audible, Bill was soon asleep.

4

The Wells Fargo truck pulled out of the Huddle House parking lot onto Route 25 heading south. Dave had stuck to their normal routine—dinner at 6:30 with his partner sitting in the truck, as per company policy, except his partner was a blow-up doll dressed in Robert's uniform. It fooled everyone.

Dave burped loudly and long as he shifted gears. His belly was as full of greasy eggs as the back of the truck was with cash. *Life is good*, he thought and *when it's this good, you don't get caught.*

He continued south hoping his two buddies were waiting for him. He preferred to call them "buddies" over "accomplices" because it didn't sound as if they were criminals and he definitely didn't think of himself as a felon.

It's funny how one's mind can justify things. Dave's mind justified his actions. He had worked for this company for 17 years and the only people making money were the bosses, or so he thought. He was going to get his share one way or another.

"Here he comes. Right on time," Mark observed as he tried to wake Sid, who had fallen asleep waiting on Dave and the truck.

"I'm awake, don't push me," Sid groaned, reaching for the keys to start the car.

"I can't believe you fell asleep. Just thinking about all that money gets me pumped up."

Mark was getting excited as the truck lumbered by. Sid just rolled his eyes. He knew the consequences if they got caught having already done two years for a B and E. They fell in behind the truck.

Crossing the train tracks, Dave could see the warehouses and the gated entrance through the rain. Dave thought, *This is perfect.* The rain and dark night would conceal their unlawful activities. Maybe they wouldn't get caught. *This feels like something out of a movie.* The truck pulled up to the gate with the car close behind. Mark got out and unlocked the gate, thinking about the money and not the rain.

Bill was startled from a deep sleep by the sound of a diesel truck stopping in front of his door.

Shit! Maybe someone is on to me. His mind started racing to find solutions to problems that would be created if he were caught. Where would he live? Would they make him move all of his stuff out? Would Steve ban him from the warehouse? How much money did he have? Maybe a motel… His mind went on and on as he sat on the edge of his bed.

Well, first things first. He got his little mirror out and poked it through the hole. *What is going on out there?*

Bill couldn't see much between the darkness and the rain, but he noticed there was a big truck parked in front of his door. It was hard for him to focus with the rain hitting the mirror. He could hear men talking and bits of their conversation, but it was muffled by the sound of a door being raised. Someone switched on the light in a bay. In the dark, the single light bulb illuminated everything with a wet glow.

Bill could see one man in a uniform and two more in jeans and rain jackets.

"Turn off that light, you dumbass!" yelled Mark to Sid.

"He'll need it to pull the truck in."

"No he won't. That's what headlights are for. Now shut it off."

"Mark, did you bring my clothes? I want to get out of this uniform," Dave asked.

Mark threw a bundle at him. "Don't turn your lights on until you get turned into the door. We don't need to draw any more attention than we already have."

Bill could hear footsteps coming towards his door. A large man filled the mirror, then turned and opened the door to the truck. The courtesy light came on and Bill could see everything—what kind of uniform the man was wearing and the name on his truck.

This set Bill to thinking. At least they weren't coming to evict him. He started putting two and two together. Three men at night, no lights, parking an armored truck in an out-of-the-way warehouse facility, worried about calling attention to themselves. It all added up to only one thing. Robbery.

5

Bill was surrounded by silence and darkness. He had heard the bay door shut and the men walk off talking among themselves. *Probably talking about how they're going to spend the money*, Bill thought. He had been afraid to move while his company was outside. The inside of Bill's space was pitch black. It was so dark Bill blinked his eyes several times, because he couldn't tell if his eyes were open or shut. His mind was going a million miles a second. Scenarios raced through his mind like race cars going by the grandstands:

Who were those guys?
Were they coming back?
Was there money in the truck?
They didn't unload any.

Maybe they already unloaded it.
Who are "they"?
Did anybody see them other than me?
When will they be back?
Should I take a look?
What time is it now?
How long should I wait?
What would I do with the money?
Is there any money in there?
What if I get caught?
Piss on that.
I've got to know.
Curiosity killed the cat.
Better to not know.
Don't kid yourself, there could be millions.
Calm down and think, you idiot.
And think he did.

First, Bill had to decide what to do. "Calm down and think," he told himself again. *I need a plan that covers all the details. A plan of action.* It amazed Bill how things slowed down as he sat by the small hole in the door thinking, watching and listening.

Sitting in the dark, Bill cleared his mind and began piecing a plan together making the decision to see what was in the truck. His subconscious decided this when he saw what kind of truck it was, but he hadn't realized it yet. He desperately needed the money and he wouldn't kid himself about that anymore.

As best as Bill could tell, his company left around 9:15 pm. He was going to wait until 2:00 am before putting the plan in motion. Bill made his way back to the bed in the dark, having no trouble navigating his small world in complete darkness. Lying on the bed he began working out the details. The only problem was trying to remain calm at the thought of all that money.

Getting the money into his truck was as far as he had got, the next step he would work out at breakfast.

***

Lying there staring into the darkness he thought, *What if there isn't any money? Well, hell, I won't be any worse off than I am now. What if the cops show up snooping around? I'll spend a few nights in my truck. Okay then, I'm going to do this.*

- Get up and change into dark clothing, black pants and shirt with a black doo rag.
- Get large bolt cutters out of toolbox
- Wear gloves at all times
- Take pistol, just in case
- Drink some water and try to relax; breathe deeply (Yeah, right.)

Bill couldn't wait and at 1:55 he raised the door enough to roll out onto the wet blacktop. He made his way down the alleyway to the door the truck was behind. *I'll take door number 318, Bob*, he thought, hoping the price was right. Placing the bolt cutters on the lock, he began to squeeze. The lock had not been properly locked and the weight of the bolt cutters popped it right open. Fate or luck? Setting down the bolt cutters, he removed the lock from the door. As Bill raised the door he half expected the truck not to be there, but the flashlight lit up the back of the grey and red truck. It was there and real. Bill couldn't believe it. He reached up and tried the handle. Locked. Nobody trusted anybody any more. He jumped up on the bumper and aimed the flashlight through the glass. He could see bags and boxes, but no money. Making his way up the side of the truck to the driver's door, he tried opening it. Locked too. Going around, he tried the passenger's door. It swung open and he could see why. A guard's uniform was lying on the seat. The belt and waist of the pants had fallen into the jamb and the door had never latched.

Bill wondered how these crooks had gotten this far. He climbed into the cab and tried to open the door to the back. It was locked. He moved to the driver's seat and sat looking into the darkness. With the flashlight, he searched for keys. No keys. For the second time in less than twelve hours, he put his hands on the steering wheel and hung his head in despair. So close, yet so far. *Well, maybe I can find another way into the back.* Bill lifted his head and thought, *If I were the driver, where would I put the keys?* He reached for the uniform and checked all the pockets of both the pants and shirt. Nothing. Maybe the ashtray. Nothing. He reached under the seat. Bill pulled out a first aid kit, but no keys. He checked the dash with the flashlight. Bare. He folded down the sun visor and a single key on a white plastic tag fell in his lap. Bingo! Without getting up, he pivoted in the seat and tried the key. It slid into the dead bolt. Holding his breath, he turned the key. The lock turned and the door slid open. Bill stuck the flashlight in and panned around the compartment.

There, piled in the back of the truck parked in an out-of-the-way storage building, was more money than Bill could have imagined. The money had been carefully wrapped in plastic cubes about twelve inches square. There were also duffel bags full with letters stenciled on them. Stepping on the money, Bill made his way to the back door and opened it. He half expected to see the police or the men who had parked the truck. Nothing greeted him but darkness and mist.

Bill walked to his truck and pulled it to the open door, never turning on his lights. Opening the rear door to the camper shell, he started loading the money. The camper shell was one of the only things he bought after Amber died. He figure if worse came to worse he could sleep in it.

First the cubes of bills went in. *What if these are all one-dollar bills?* But by that point there was no caring. There were thousands of bills and either way, he would be richer than an hour ago. He grabbed the first of many duffel bags and slung it into the back of his truck. After a few more, he grabbed one that was considerably heavier than the others. Coins. *Maybe I should leave it,* he thought. *Nah, money's money.* A slight smile crossed his face.

Bill finished emptying the armored truck. He stopped for the first time to look around and realized he had been concentrating so much on the transfer of the money he hadn't noticed anything around him. The slim flashlight offered little illumination as he checked his surroundings. The light rain and mist cut down on visibility. Bill thought he must be almost invisible from more than twenty feet away. He couldn't see anyone; no one could see him.

Time to finish and get out of here. Bill took a moment, shut off the flashlight and went over things in his mind. Standing in the dark, the only sound was water hitting the bottom of the downspout.

He took the pants of the uniform and tied the legs together to form a bag. Using the shirt, he brushed out the back of the truck, hoping not to leave any incriminating evidence. Everything then went into the makeshift bag. He locked all the doors to the truck and pulled down the roll-up door. Putting the key in the bag, he deposited it in the dumpster. Man, was somebody going to be surprised! *Only a few more things to do and then I'm going to get some breakfast.* Moving that much money was hard work.

Bill went back to his pod to put up his tools and to get some superglue. He returned to the bay where the armored truck was and double-checked the padlock. After finding the lock on the crooks' door open, he would double check padlocks for the rest of his life. Bill then filled the key opening to the padlock with super glue, so no one would have a chance of unlocking it. He was feeling giddy as he left the complex.

6

At 4:00 am on a rainy morning, there aren't many cars on the road. Bill's stomach rumbled as he sat waiting for the light to turn green. He waited and waited although there wasn't any sign of another car. He thought about going through it; thought about it, but decided against it. If a cop came out of nowhere and pulled him over, he would have a greater chance of being caught with the load of "inherited money"

"Hell," and he put the truck in gear. "I could be a millionaire if I don't get caught. Just don't do anything stupid." He put the truck in neutral and waited some more. Bill began thinking about every move he had to make. Somebody was going to be really pissed off when they got back to their warehouse. The truck was empty of everything.

The big question he had been pondering was about the money. You can't just open up a bank account with that amount of cash. That would draw more than a little attention.

The light was finally green and Bill was on his way to Waffle House. After pulling into the parking lot he checked his wallet. Even with a pickup truck load of cash, he wanted to make sure he could pay for breakfast. Then Bill chuckled at the irony of his actions.

"Good morning," said the waitress as he walked through the door. The place was bright with light but had a dim feeling of exhaustion. Bill sat in a booth with a sign that read, "Booths reserved for two or more guests." He didn't care, though; he was the only one in the restaurant.

The waitress was an older woman with bad teeth. Maybe she wasn't that old; maybe she was just ridden hard or had a tough life. The cook, on the other hand, was young, tall and thin. Bill couldn't tell if his Elvis hairstyle was greasy from the grill or gel.

"Do you know what you want or need a minute?" asked the waitress.

"Coffee and let me think."

She was off to get the coffee. Returning with a heavy porcelain mug, she looked at Bill as if she didn't have all night, well, morning, to take his order.

"Let's see, I'll have the cheese and eggs, toast, grits and bacon..." his voice trailed off as he glanced outside at another car coming into the parking lot.

A county deputy's black and white Charger pulled into a slot facing the street. Bill's heart began to speed up. There was no way they could have known what had transpired that night. But he still had that feeling of guilt beginning to haunt him.

The waitress yelled out Bill's order to the cook in some kind of Waffle House code. It snapped Bill back to reality.

Bill tried to focus on something, anything else other than the crime he had committed. He began to prepare his coffee as the cop came in and sat at the counter. The deputy saw Bill and they made eye contact. The men nodded at each other. The waitress was already putting a cup of coffee in front of the deputy.

"You want your usual?" she asked the young lawman.

With that comment, Bill knew this must be something the deputy did every morning, or at least when he worked nights. Bill relaxed a bit and went back to thinking about the money. *What am I going to do with it?* The first thing would be to count it, but that's not something he could do in a parking lot and certainly not back at the warehouse. *Where then? Someplace where I won't be bothered or seen. Maybe I should rent another storage building.* That was one possibility. *Someplace private and out of the way.*

Bill tried to concentrate. The cop sure wasn't helping things. He had a lot of money in the back of his truck and a cop was sitting twenty feet from it. The anxiety was steadily eating away at him.. Not only were the guys who stole it going to be looking for him, but so was the law. What to do? The possibilities were endless.

The waitress poured more coffee in Bill's mug.

"You traveling?" the waitress asked.

The question broke his train of thought.

"I wish. I've got work. Have to be in early for a shut-down at a plant."

What Bill told her was the truth, but he planned to call in sick.

"Yeah, it's a bitch to work for a living. If I didn't have two grandkids at the house I wouldn't be here."

"And if I didn't have a house payment, car payment and didn't have to eat I wouldn't be here," the deputy piped up.

Bill looked at the young officer and said, "Hell, I thought all you guys were on the take and had plenty of cash." He smiled at the deputy. The man knew Bill was joking and smiled back.

"Sometimes I wonder if that wouldn't be easier... I'll deny I ever said that, though," and they all laughed out loud.

Bill finished his meal and walked to the register to pay. He threw two dollars down on the table, then picked it up and put a ten down. He could afford to be generous now. As he turned to leave, his eyes met with the deputy's again.

"I'll see you later," Bill said, "and be careful out there."

"Thanks."

7

The rain and mist had stopped as Bill headed to Wal-Mart, but it was still dark out. The parking lot was empty except for a few cars parked along the fence. Bill counted 25 spots with the blue and white wheelchair signs as he approached the entrance. Wal-Mart must expect every handicapped person in Hendersonville to shop here at the same time. He grabbed a cart and pushed on into the store. The glare of the lights made him squint as he looked around. *What? No happy greeter at 5:30 in the morning?* he thought. He had already made a mental list of things he needed but still decided to browse several rows.

Bill was not a regular Wal-Mart shopper. Everybody always complained about it being crowded, but he must have found the perfect time to shop. There were only a few customers and the clerks looked worn out. No one really noticed Bill. Perfect. He began putting things in the cart: small buckets, a calculator, plastic bags, pencils and pads. Things that looked random, but all had a purpose.

When Bill left Wal-Mart, he knew exactly where to go. A few years back, Bill and Amber had been to a party at a friend's house that was on top of a mountain in a small subdivision.

Some subdivision, Bill thought as he drove up the steep, gravel road. He didn't pass a house for the first mile. He came to a fork in the road at a cluster of four houses and made a right turn. The road got steeper with more switchbacks. This was only the second time Bill had been up this road and he began doubting his sense of direction. Another mile and he came to another fork. Staying left this time he remembered the hill. Last time his truck spun gravel going up and it did just the same this time too. At the crest of the hill, he saw what he was looking for: a faded "For Sale" sign with the name of the real estate company and a smaller sign reading "6.4 acres". Someone had started a driveway into the property. It was overgrown, but the chain across it was still intact.

Even the Walmart brand of bolt cutters made short work of the lock. Bill pulled in and put his own lock on the chain. The drive went up a small rise and then down to a clearing about one hundred yards off the road.

As he parked the truck, the sun was starting to rise, but a thick fog had developed from the night's rain. Bill put his seat back and made himself comfortable. It wasn't long before he dozed off.

He awoke to a tapping noise outside his window. Slowly raising his eyelids, he half expected to see someone standing at the truck. The tapping continued. Moving his eyes only, Bill saw a blue jay perched on top of his mirror, bending over and pecking at it. Looking at the digital clock on the radio, he had slept longer than planned. *What a night. It's tiring stealing someone else's stolen money. Time to see how much I've inherited.*

***

Opening the rear door to the camper, Bill stood looking at the mess. *This just won't do.* Everything was a jumble. Wal-Mart bags, green duffel bags and square bundles in brown paper and plastic. If anyone, had looked in they wouldn't have suspected a thing. The mess made Bill cringe. To him, everything needed to be shipshape and stored away.

First things first. Bill set up a ten-foot square sunshade and backed the truck under it. He let the tailgate down and unfolded a beach chair. Fifteen minutes later, all the Wal-Mart stuff was set up and arranged: a calculator, pad and pencils lay on a small plastic table. Bill was ready and pulled the first cube of money out.

Carefully cutting the brown paper to reveal the money inside, Bill almost fainted. His heart began to pound as he tried to stay seated in the beach chair. Catching his breath, he looked again at the cube of money.

It was full of twenty-dollar bills that were banded in $1,000 packs. Once he got his wits about him, the counting began.

There were twelve layers, $9,000 to a layer. Bill did the math several times. $96,000. He thought he was going to have a heart attack. Looking inside the truck, his eyes saw many of the brown squares. *Find a paper bag to breathe into; you're going to hyperventilate.*

After the initial shock, Bill carefully wrapped the paper back around the brick of money. He marked the outside of the package with a big, block "C" for counted. Setting the counted bundle aside, he grabbed another one. There were twenties in this one also. Taped and marked, he set it with the other one. The third one was a surprise. It had hundreds marked in $5,000 packets. Bill did the calculations over and over and it always came up the same. $540,000. A half a million dollars! He had to take a dump.

After the intermission, he sat in the lawn chair and tried to compose himself. Again, the thought came to him that there were going to be some pissed off people. Bill's mind played the scene of those fellows coming back to their truck over and over in his head. Well, it wasn't really their truck. It was just in their possession. Bill began thinking he had to play this right. *Use your head and think. Don't react.* He knew the law would be around sooner or later and the men who stole the truck would be looking for the money. Well, as for right now, nobody would suspect him. No one knew he lived in the warehouse or had been there when the truck arrived. But what about all this money? He looked into the back of the truck, took a deep breath and began counting again. One thing at a time.

Bill tried to count all the wrapped notes first. Just as he thought the last cube was counted, another one would be found under a duffel bag. Most of the bundles had been hundred dollar bills. The cubes had been counted and wrapped up in a plastic trash bag, at least two to a bag. As he taped up the last one, it dawned on him that the bills had all been in circulation, no new notes.

Bill started on the duffel bag, opening it and looking inside. This was going to be a job, a jumble of fives, tens and twenties banded together in packs. Bill set up trash bags and began sorting the cash.

In the bottom of the duffel bags, there were boxes of rolled coins. He broke open each roll into a gallon bucket. The first duffel held close to $300,000. So far Bill had counted over $8 million. He wasn't going to count the change, but he had a bunch of buckets. Then he heard a vehicle on the road.

Keeping low, Bill ran towards the dirt road. From the brush he saw an AMC Eagle station wagon drive by the chained off driveway. Bill watched as it drove another couple hundred yards to the cul-de-sac and turned around. It drove slowly past the last and only house. Obviously the driver was looking for something, maybe Bill. The driver looked at the chain as he drove by, but didn't stop. Bill was grateful for the peace and quiet of his surroundings. It allowed him to hear the car descend the road for a long time.

After what Bill figured was enough time on the lookout, he confidently returned to the truck. Coming down the drive towards his truck, he could observe the setup. It looked odd from a distance, all that man-made stuff surrounded by nature. Looking in the back of the truck, Bill figured he was a little better than halfway done. Counting the money was taking longer than he thought. Time for lunch.

8

Once the counting had been completed, Bill dug a large hole and buried the money. Before depositing the money in the hole, he made sure each bag was watertight with duct tape, ensuring the money wouldn't rot. Although, all money rots one way or another.

First stop after the burial was the real estate office listing the lot. No point in hiding money on property you didn't own. It was very close to closing time and the agent was nice enough to not rush Bill out. The agent made an appointment for them to meet in the morning, which Bill thought was unusual, considering it was Saturday.

Leaving the real estate office, Bill drove to the bank in Hendersonville. He deposited $1,500, a small amount, considering the amount of money he had "fallen into." Why draw attention to yourself with a large deposit?

Now his work began in earnest. Bill drove to the closest grocery store to cash in the coins. He began by using the automated coin exchange at each store, only cashing in $200-$300 at each machine, again not wanting to call attention to himself. After visiting all the stores in Hendersonville, Bill felt pretty good about things as he drove down the interstate towards Greenville, hoping to find more coin exchange stations.

Around 8:00 PM Bill started to run out of steam. He found a small mom and pop motel to recuperate and plan for tomorrow. By the time he was finished showering, the pizza delivery boy was knocking on the door. With the TV on low and a slice of pizza in his hand, Bill spread the loose cash on the second bed. There was more cash than he earned in a month working, although counting and changing the coins into cash was harder work than he thought. Lying back on the bed, Bill was soon fast asleep.

The next morning he showered again, then counted all the cash he had exchanged, plus what was in the packets he hadn't buried: $7,230. That was the most cash Bill had ever had at one time in his life. He stopped at a few more coin exchanges on his way back to meet the realtor.

On the drive back to Hendersonville, Bill began thinking. He had millions of dollars, most of it buried.

What should I do with it? He surely didn't want to get caught by the law or the guys who stole it, either one of which wouldn't be healthy. He also didn't want to end up like those people who win the lotteries— broke, in debt and miserable. The best thing would be to play it cool, taking time to think about every move. Maybe do the right thing for a change. *Think, don't react.* The right thing would be to turn the money back in, but that wasn't going to happen. Somehow Bill was going to have to get some, or most, of the money into a bank... or banks. He could see himself going into his bank now. "I've got several million I need to deposit." The teller would panic. Bill knew that any deposit over $10,000 in cash would look suspicious and set off alarms. Well, at least that's what he had heard. Bill started doing the math in his head. If I deposited $5,000 a day, how long would it take to deposit $1 million, times the number of millions he had? Word problems. He hated them in school and he still hated them, only this one was important. After pulling over to the side of the road, Bill hunted for his calculator. Taking into account bank holidays and weekends, it would take eleven years to get all the cash in a bank. Bill laughed out loud at that idea. *Forget that. Well, hell, first things first. I need a place to live.* And he drove on.

The real estate agent was okay for a salesman, but a little too hyper for Bill. As the agent drove to Sky View Acres, he described the property. Bill sat quietly as the agent pressed on about the lot. There were 6.4 acres and the owner had already drilled a well. A septic system had also been installed for a three-bedroom house. Bill just listened as the agent continued to talk up the lot. He tuned out the agent's sales pitch and his mind began to wander. *Have I missed anything? Are all the details covered? Does anybody have any idea what I've done? Will anybody figure it out?* Bill tried to recall all the things that had taken place in the last 36 hours. *Have I messed up anywhere?* That was the nagging question he asked himself time and time again.

"There is a small fee for road upkeep and just a few restrictions, nothing major," the agent said as Bill came back to reality.

They parked in front of the chain and Cam, the agent, tried to unlock the lock. Bill sat in the car watching this poor man struggle with the lock, knowing full well his key wouldn't work. Bill had changed locks.

"Hmm, the owner must have sent me the wrong key. I guess we'll have to walk from here," Cam shouted to Bill.

The two men spent several hours walking the property. Cam pointed out the wellhead. Bill maneuvered Cam so that he was standing directly over the buried money. They stood there for several minutes like chickens scratching the ground. Cam never noticed anything. Another car pulled up and parked and a man appeared at the gate.

"Hey Cam," the older man called to the agent. "I thought that was you coming up here. I just wanted to make sure. You can never be too careful."

Cam looked like a deer in the headlights. This man had caused Cam's last two prospects to shy away from this lot. Selling real estate was a dog-eat-dog job. Trying to sell lots up here was almost impossible because of the road and remoteness. Then there was this idiot, who thought he was the mayor of the subdivision. He bullied everyone who lived here or wanted to live here.

The man walked up to Bill saying, "Hi, I'm Frank Skeeter."

Bill didn't say a word. He just looked the man up and down. A small, sly smile flashed across his face as he thought, *Skeeter, as in, "There's a skeeter on my peter, knock it off, knock it off."*

"I live in the house at the first Y in the road," Skeeter said with his hand still extended towards Bill. Skeeter was starting to feel uncomfortable standing in front of Bill with his hand extended. Just as he was about to drop it, Bill grabbed it and the two of them shook hands. It was a very awkward moment for Frank and Cam as they looked at each other.

"You thinking about buying this lot, son?" Skeeter asked Bill.

Another long, awkward moment passed before Bill answered.

"Maybe, dad," Bill finally said.

Cam knew he had to say something. "Well, we were just going back to my office to talk about that, weren't we…", Cam trailed off as he headed towards his car. Bill didn't follow. He continued to stare at Skeeter. Frank was beginning to feel a real unease. Usually Frank was the one making someone else uncomfortable, but not this time.

Skeeter broke the strained silence between the two. "The bank won't loan much on this land. Why don't you come back before you make your decision and I'll give you the skinny on living up here."

The car started up and Bill looked over at Cam. He was waving for him to come on. Bill started for the car without a word. Frank followed like a small dog. Bill reached the car and opened the door. Frank put his hand on Bill's shoulder. Bill recoiled like a snake and stared at Frank's hand.

"We really need to talk, young fellow," Frank said as Bill reached around and peeled the hand from his shoulder and threw it down. Finally Bill spoke. "I really don't care what you have to say. I'll make up my own mind and don't ever touch me again." There was so much malice in Bill's voice that Frank took two steps back because he thought he was going to get hit. Bill looked in the car at Cam and said, "Do they spray for skeeters up here in the summer?"

With that Bill got in the car and Cam backed out onto the road. He had to gently maneuver around Skeeter's AMC stationwagon. Neither Bill nor Cam said anything until they got to the paved road.

"He thinks he's the mayor up there," Cam said, trying to lighten things up. "I guess that's okay, being he keeps an eye on everything."

Not on everything, Bill thought.

Cam continued fishing, "So what did you think about the property?"

Bill sat and thought a minute before saying anything. "Well, it's definitely out of the way. The road could be a problem, especially in the winter. And then there's your buddy, Mr. Skeeter. He sure is a nosy rosy."

Cam didn't like where this was going. He had to change the direction of the conversation.

"What kind of work do you do?" Cam asked.

"Sheet metal. How much are they asking for the lot?"

Cam hesitated and then said, "The owner is asking $49,500, but he told me to bring all offers."

No response from Bill. He just sat there thinking. *If I don't dicker on the price it might set off alarms. The land is perfect and Skeeter will be a minor problem, just like a real skeeter. If Cam knew I could pay cash a hundred times over, he'd shit.*

Cam parked the car and shut off the ignition. He sat looking out the windshield. *That damned Skeeter ran off another buyer. I've got to have a talk with him. I'll*

never sell a lot up there with him putting in his two cents.
Cam looked at Bill. *This guy's a waste of time anyway.*
Look at him; he doesn't have any money and probably has
no credit. This job sucks.

"I'll make an offer."

"What!" It took Cam by surprise. He had to
hear it again.

"I said I'll make an offer."

"Ah, that's great. I'll try and do everything I can to
make this happen."

Cam couldn't believe it. The houses or lots hardly
ever sold in Sky View Acres. This would be a feather
in his hat. All the agents made fun of this subdivision
or anyone showing a lot there. This was a testament
to his selling ability, too bad he didn't know the truth
of the matter. To him, with the road and Mr. Skeeter,
this was almost a miracle.

The two men sat across from each other in Cam's
small office. Spread on his desk were all the papers
and plats for the land. Cam looked like a rat waiting
for a large meal instead of Bill's offer.

Bill started, "Considering that most of the lot is too
steep to build on, the road and, of course, Skeeter, the
best I could offer is $30,000 and that's only because it
already has a well and septic."

Cam was happy that it wasn't much lower.

"That's way below the asking price, but I'll take it to
the owner." *Damn right, I'll take it to the owner.* It's the

only offer he's had on it in two years. The last people to look at it made Cam turn around halfway up the road. "I'll let you know something on Tuesday."

No, get him on the phone now. I want to hammer out this deal today

"But that's…"

"No buts. Call him, or the deal's off," Bill insisted.

"This is unusual, but let me ask you some questions first. Are you going through a bank?"

"No, cash on the barrel head." And, Bill thought, *I do mean cash* and grinned.

"I'll want to close within thirty days or less. I'll pay for the survey, if we can reach a deal today. One more thing, I'll need to put a storage building up there immediately."

"I've got to check with the seller on that one. Maybe if you put a large deposit down he'll go for that."

"Is $7,500 large enough? And if something falls through he can keep it."

"Can I put that in writing?" Cam asked.

Bill just nodded.

Cam reached the seller after several calls. They closed the deal before Bill left the office. Everyone was satisfied, but only Bill knew it was all just a game.

9

Everything was looking good. The weather had cleared and Bill now owned the property where the money was buried. Almost. Life was good. It was amazing how easy things were when you had money to back you up. Lots and lots of money.

Saturday was a big day at the Home Depot, but even then, it was still not that busy. That's why Bill went there instead of Lowe's.

He slowly walked about the sheds that were prebuilt in the parking lot. He inspected each one to see if it would meet his needs. About halfway through his search, a salesman approached Bill.

"Can I help you, sir?"

"I think so. I need a small building and that eight by twenty seems like the one that'll work. Can you do any better on the price?" Bill asked the salesman.

"If you open up a Home Depot credit card I can give you ten percent off."

"I'll tell you what. Give me 20 percent off and I'll take it."

"Only the manager can do that. Let me check." The salesman pulled out a phone and walked out into the parking lot. After talking for a few seconds, he said, "The best we can do is 15, sir."

Bill walked around the building, knocking on the walls and then went inside. "Okay, if you can deliver it today."

"Sorry, we can't deliver it until Monday."

"Can I borrow your phone?" Bill reached out his hand toward the salesman.

He dialed Fred's number from memory. As he was dialing, he thought, *I need to get me one of these*. He had refused to buy a cell phone in the past because he felt as if he didn't need it, but now that he could afford one, it felt necessary to have one. Fred answered on the third ring.

"Hi Fred, this is Bill."

"What's up? Been awhile."

"Yeah, sorry about that, but with everything that's been going on and no phone it's hard keeping up."

"No problems, man."

"Anyway, I bought a lot in Sky View Acres, not far from your old place and I need to get a storage shed up there. You once bragged that the fellow you worked for could do anything and I was wondering if he could help me out. I'm at Home Depot right now and I want to get this thing up there today."

"That's funny, man, we're in Home Depot, too. We'll be right out," Fred told Bill.

Bill could hear Fred shouting his name from across the parking lot. Bill waved at the two men coming toward him. Fred hadn't changed since the last time they saw each other, hair unkempt, maybe a little greyer, beard and bright blue eyes. The other fellow lagged several steps behind. Not as tall as Fred, but not so heavy, either. *This must be Scott*, Bill thought. Fred had spoken highly of Scott the night of the party, but what had stuck in Bill's mind was when Fred had said, "Scott is of a different sort." Fred could not explain it very well, but Bill got his meaning just the same. Looking at Scott now, Bill fully understood Fred's statement. Scott's eyes scanned the parking lot and settled on Bill—looking him over. Bill shifted his weight and he could see Scott's body react. It was as if right below the surface a wild animal was lurking.

"So you bought a lot in Sky View Acres. You idiot! Nobody lives up there but wackos…" Fred laughed. "Just kidding. I loved it up there. Which lot did you get?"

"You know the last hill you crest before going down to your old place?"

Fred nodded.

"Well, right there."

"Shoot man, that's more than a lot! There must be four or five acres in there! You going to build up there?"

"Maybe, but I need to get this building up there first. And I want it today. You think you can help me out?"

"It's a helluva coincidence, Bill. This here is Scott. I just started back working for him. I've been gone awhile since my divorce and all, but he was nice enough to gimme my job back when I decided to get my life back together again." Fred turned to Scott. "Scott, this is Bill."

Fred stood back as he introduced the two men. He had known Scott for years, yet he still never knew what Scott would say or do.

"Nice to meet you, Bill. Fred has told me a lot about you," Scott said as he stuck out his hand.

"Don't worry. Fred told me a lot about you, too," Bill replied as they shook hands, each man wondering what the other knew about him.

"Well, can we get this building up there today?" Bill asked.

"It ain't going to be an easy job," Scott warned, eyeing the building.

"I'm willing to pay cash if you can make it happen today."

"How much?" Scott inquired.

"You tell me. I don't know what you're worth."

Scott scratched his chin and thought a moment. "I'll tell you what. You pay Fred and I'll only charge you $50 an hour. That includes all equipment and rigging."

Bill stuck out his hand and agreed, "Done. I'll go in and pay for it and we'll get started."

"We're running out of daylight. To save some time, me and Fred will go and get the dozer. We'll come back here and get you and the building," Scott suggested.

"That works for me, because I still need to get some other stuff," Bill answered as he headed into the store."

Scott and Fred took off to get the dozer at Scott's shop. Both men were happy to get the work. Business had been slow since 9/11 and with winter coming on, everything slowed down. They loaded the dozer and took it out to the bottom of the road at Sky View Acres, then drove back to get Bill.

Bill was waiting in front of the shed with the salesman. The salesman started in on Bill—trying to get more money out of him.

"We have a crew to move these buildings. That's all they do and they're good at it. I'm sure you would save a lot of money…" Blah, blah, blah, blah. The salesman went on and on. What he didn't say was that the moving company gave the salesman $100 in kickback for every building they moved. "Do you want me to call them?" the salesman suggested as he started to dial his cell.

"No," Bill groaned, sounding bored. The salesman started interrogating Bill again, but Bill cut him off. "What part of NO don't you understand?" They made eye contact and Bill just glared at him until he moved off in the direction of the store.

Scott and Fred pulled the building up onto the trailer using the winch. The shed was ten feet wide not eight and overhung the sides of the trailer. It didn't weigh much and luckily pulled well going down the road. Scott and Bill were in the dump truck towing the building with Fred following behind with his flashers on. Traffic was heavy with all the leaf-lookers in town and such.

"Have you known Fred long?" Bill asked Scott.

"Since before Big Ben died. How do you know him?" Scott asked as he checked his mirrors to see how the trailer was doing.

"A friend took me and my girlfriend to a party he was having on the mountain two summers ago."

Scott didn't respond. He knew which party Bill was talking about. Scott had stopped drinking and partying years back. A lot of things changed when he started dating his future wife. She was and had been a church-going person her whole life and when Scott started dating her she told him he would have to go, too. He had already stopped drinking about a year before when his live-in girlfriend left him, but church was a new adventure for him. Scott didn't even think about going to parties any more, though. Why tempt himself? In fact, once he started going to church, a lot of his old friends seemed to disappear from his life except Fred.

Fred and Scott met each other through Big Ben. Ben was trying to start a motorcycle shop, but it was a slow process, so he welded on the side for Scott. He also sold some dope, mostly pills, but he never had much cash—even with his extra income.

Scott never liked going to Ben's house because he never knew who was going to show up. He made it a point never to go around dinnertime due to the place being overall disgusting. However, despite all of Ben's downsides, he was a decent welder and it helped both of them out.

Ben and Fred were childhood friends, so it was just a matter of time before Fred and Scott met each other. Ben had always tried to live the outlaw-biker life, but never quite made it. Sure, he rode a Harley, partied hard and worked on motorcycles, but he also had two little girls and a wife with a house. He was always looking for that big score. Basically, he was a white Southern redneck, but he was a good friend and would always be available when someone needed him.

Scott, on the other hand, was more of the lone biker. He had lived closer to the image of the biker life than anybody knew.

Then there was Fred. After several divorces and a bankruptcy, he was living with his mother. Enough said.

All these thoughts and memories went through Scott's head in seconds. He turned to Bill and declared, "Old Fred, he never seems to figure it out."

"I know what you mean." This time Bill checked the mirror to eye the trailer.

"You got much work going on?" Bill asked.

"Not much. We finished a good-sized job at some schools right after 9/11 and it's been week to week after that. I've laid off everybody but Fred and the Mexican. I don't know what's going to happen. How about you?"

"We're slow, but I've been getting forty in." Bill didn't even want to mention 9/11. "I'm going to start building a house. Maybe you can give me a hand. It's not what you all do, but it's work, just the same."

Scott looked at Bill and grinned. "Didn't Fred tell you? We're whores. We'll do anything for money."

They both laughed. "No he didn't say that, but he did say you could do almost anything."

"I don't know about that." Scott didn't like people bragging on him.

"He thinks highly of you, said you come through when the chips are down. I can take you at your word."

"Don't blow smoke up my ass. What do you want?"

"Nothing. I'm just telling you what he said."

"Great. He was probably drunk," Scott grumbled, thinking about what else Fred might have said about him. There were a few things Fred knew about Scott that were better left unsaid.

Bill continued, "I'm going out of town next week, when I get back let's see if we can talk some business. I'd like to have the house in the dry before Christmas."

"It's going to be hard to get money from the bank for a house up there," Scott told him.

"I just got some money from an inheritance. Not a lot, but enough for a small house," Bill affirmed, hoping Scott couldn't tell it was a lie.

Bill eyed Scott one more time, trying to size him up. Scott was somewhere in his forties, in good physical shape, with black hair and a short beard. He didn't give much away. He had experienced a lot of life and preferred to keep to himself. Scott had few friends, but if he took to you, he would treat you like a brother.

Using the dozer to pull the trailer, the three men finally made it up the steep road. Once at the lot, they all agreed a truck would never have made the pull. It was a beautiful afternoon with blue skies and temperatures in the high sixties.

With the building off the trailer, Fred and Scott leveled it using cement block and wood shims. Bill unloaded his truck and covered the material with plastic. Scott decided to leave the trailer and dozer on the lot for now—they would need it to clear a building site if an agreement could be reached.

On the way back to town, Fred filled in Scott about Bill and how his girlfriend had gotten killed on 9/11. Fred expressed that it had been a shame, as she was so good looking.

Fred teased, "What's really a killer, was the night of the party. I kept hitting on her and she kept blowing me off."

"I can't imagine that, since you're such a Don Juan. I don't know how women resist you."

"Me neither."

"Let's see, being forty-three and still living with your mother, I'm sure that doesn't have anything to do with it. Neither does being divorced twice and having no money, among a dozen other qualities."

"Has anyone told you you're an asshole lately?"

Both men laughed.

"Well, better to be an asshole than sleep with Dottie," Scott said. Dottie was Ben's wife, maybe ex-wife. Nobody knew for sure, but a real skank.

"We got any work for Monday?" Fred changed the subject. Scott's last comment hit too close to the bone for him.

"No, me and Taco Boy are going to the church to change filters and he has some insulation to put on. That's about it."

"Well, I'll work on Mom's house, try and get it ready for winter. She's got a honey-do list a mile long."

"Some honey she's got," Scott looked over at Fred. "You better keep her happy, or you'll be living under a bridge this winter."

"Naw, she's my mother. A bitch, but still my mother."

No comment from Scott. He didn't want to open that can of worms.

"Maybe the work your buddy Bill wants to talk about will pan out."

"Let's hope so, or it'll be a long winter."

10

Bill made one more trip to Home Depot that evening. He grabbed a bite to eat before going back up the mountain. He realized he was going to have to be more organized if he was to live up here. It took twenty minutes to get from his property to the paved road, then another twenty to get to town.

It was starting to get dark as he locked the chain behind him. He pulled a sleeping bag and air mattress from the truck. It was kind of depressing to sleep on the floor with only an electric lantern for light, but with a little work this could be very livable until the house was completed. Lying in his sleeping bag, he began to sketch a floor plan for the house. He fell asleep making notes of things that needed to be done. It had been a long day and he slept well.

The next morning, Bill awoke to sunshine and birds singing. He lay in his makeshift bed thinking about where to go or what to do first.

It was Sunday and he thought of Scott going to church. *That's what I should be doing, but I won't go by myself. Maybe Scott would invite me.* Bill got up and dressed. Once outside, he realized it was a perfect day to go riding. He stopped for a moment and listened. *Yep*, he thought. The parkway was calling.

There wasn't anyone at the warehouse as he pushed his motorcycle from the building, but that shouldn't have been a surprise. There never was. He was glad there wasn't. Either no one had come back for the money or… he didn't want to think about the options. Nothing seemed amiss as he left.

In actuality, the armored truck thieves wouldn't be back. The law would, they had gotten caught.

Bill met some friends at Pisgah Inn whom he hadn't seen since Amber died. It made him feel warm and depressed at the same time. The group left the inn and rode together up the parkway. Bill's BMW was a 750cc and he noticed that without Amber on the back he didn't have to push as hard to stay with the group. He still missed her terribly. *I should have married her.* All kinds of things went through his mind. Maybe riding wasn't such a good idea.

The group stopped at an overlook for a rest. Everybody was glad to see Bill again and told him they were sorry for his loss. He admitted it was hard, but he was trying to move forward with his life. As everyone was catching up, a lone rider pulled in on a BMW that looked different but the same. Getting off the bike, the rider removed his helmet. Bill recognized Scott.

One of the other riders, Ricky, also recognized Scott and walked over and shook hands with him. Scott used to ride with their group awhile back. In fact, Scott was one of the original members of the breakfast club, as they informally referred to themselves. As the group grew more and more, Scott felt as if the karma wasn't there anymore. Not being a team player, he moved on to become a solitary rider.

Scott turned as Bill called out his name.

"Bill," Scott nodded. "Kind of surprised to see you here. I didn't know you rode. Fred never said anything about you having a bike."

"Two actually. Bad habits."

"I know what you mean."

"What are you riding?" Bill asked.

"It's a 750 I put together from a bunch of parts we had left over from my son's bike."

All three riders stood and looked over the motorcycle. From a bunch of leftover parts, Scott had constructed a very nice motorcycle. It was a mixture of different years and models. That was the beauty of older BMW's— a lot of parts interchanged.

Scott broke the silence. "I was asking Ricky if he could work his magic on the front end. There's a wobble when I go into a turn, so it's a little unsettling at times."

"That's an understatement," Ricky claimed. He was also one of the first riders in the breakfast club.

"So what are you riding, Bill," Scott asked?

The three walked over to Bill's bike, while Scott and Ricky were talking about old times and friends.

Scott was looking over the motorcycle as some of the riders pulled out. Bill made no attempt to follow them. Ricky waved and blew his horn as he exited the overlook. Then it was quiet except for the whine of motorcycles accelerating up the road.

Bill looked at Scott and said, "So much for waiting on me."

"I guess they figure you can catch up. That's what's nice about that group, every man for himself. What year is your bike?"

Bill couldn't tell if Scott was being sarcastic or not.

"It's a '75. I think it's the last year BMW made the 750, but I'm not sure."

"Pretty nice." Scott turned and walked towards his bike.

"Hey Scott, if you got a minute, I want to talk about starting the house."

Scott looked at his watch. He had been riding for two hours and covered a lot of miles. Maybe it was time for a break. Scott usually didn't talk business on a Sunday, but he sorely needed the work. And besides, it was time to find out if this guy was for real or not. Bill couldn't be too bad; he rode the same kind of bike. Then again, Scott had met some strange people on motorcycles.

"Okay," Scott said as he turned around.

Bill pushed his bike into the shade with Scott's and they sat in a grassy spot at the overlook. The view was spectacular. At this altitude, the trees were at their peak color. The temperature was in the sixties and the cloudless sky was a perfect Carolina blue.

Scott looked out at the view for a long time before speaking. He couldn't help thinking about Anne, his former girlfriend and the number of hours they had spent at this overlook. But that was another lifetime ago.

"Let's talk," Scott said.

The two men talked for over an hour. Most would have said it was just a bull session. It was more, two men feeling each other out. Bill told Scott all about Amber and his life afterwards. Scott held his cards tighter to the vest. So many people had burned him, it taught him to be cautious. The more Bill and Scott talked, the more each realized the other was a no bullshit kind of guy.

Before parting, Scott had agreed to finish the interior of the storage building. Both men left with confidence that each was a man of his word.

11

Monday morning Bill drove to work thinking things were going pretty well. That was until he got there. There was a note for him to see Brian Daniels before going to the jobsite. He waited on the loading dock until he saw Daniels pull up in his Tahoe.

"My office. Now." Daniels demanded, loud enough for everyone around to hear it.

Bill put his finger to his chest. "You mean me?"

The question caught Daniels by surprise.

"Didn't you see my note?"

"No, I didn't get that memo," Bill lied.

Everyone standing on the dock or in the bay was now listening to the exchange. They all knew Bill could be a smartass, but he could afford to be in more ways than one. He was one of the best mechanics in the business.

"Just get in my office." Daniels had no intention of verbally fencing with this guy. It was a losing battle, because he knew Bill didn't give a shit.

Bill entered the office and plopped down in a chair. Brian took this as a sign of disrespect. It was and it wasn't. Nobody respected Brian because he was so arrogant and bossy. Brian was an estimator and project manager, but you would have thought he was a god. He definitely thought so.

"Where were you Friday and Saturday?" Brian asked sitting down at his desk.

"I called in. Something important came up and I couldn't make it," Bill told him. And then he thought, *something like $16 or $17 million* and a smile crossed his face.

"You think this is funny? Well it won't be funny when you're working twelve to fourteen hours every day this week to catch up," Brian said with a smile.

"Well, first off, I can't work overtime this week and second, you can't force me to," Bill stated.

"Well, let me tell you something, you will work those hours, or you won't have a job."

That was what Bill was waiting for and he got up from the chair and headed for the door.

"Sit down. I'm not finished talking to you."

Bill turned. "I'm finished with you. In fact, I'm finished with you forever, dickhead."

Brian's mouth moved up and down, but no sound came out. Bill was halfway down the hall when he heard, "Get your tools off my truck! You don't work here anymore and I'll see to it you don't work anywhere anymore!" Brian kept on and on, but Bill just ignored it. Without turning around he threw up his arm and gave Daniels the one finger salute. Bill knew if he played things right he would never have to deal with someone like this again.

The owner of the company couldn't help but hear all the fuss Brian was raising.

"What was that all about?" Mr. Arthur asked Brian.

"I just fired Bill August for not showing up on Friday or Saturday."

"You can't fire someone for not working overtime. If he goes to the Labor Board or causes trouble, you're gone too."

"Don't worry. He'll be back, begging me for a job. I know him. He has to work."

"You better hope so. He was one of our best field men. All the men like him and respect him. More than I can say for you," the owner told Brian. Mr. Arthur had been looking for a way to get rid of this arrogant asshole and it looked like he had found it.

As Mr. Arthur finished letting Brian know where he stood, Bill came through the door. Bill stuck out his hand to Mr. Arthur. "It's been good working for you. Sorry things didn't work out."

"Well, if you need a job come back and see me," and Mr. Arthur shook Bill's hand.

"As long as he's here, I won't be back," Bill confessed to Mr. Arthur. He looked at Brian and winked. Bill left knowing that was the last day he would ever work for someone else.

Mr. Arthur turned to Brian. "You're an idiot. He won't be back," and walked off. Brian stood watching Bill leave the parking lot, thinking, *He'll be back.*

Bill pulled out of the parking lot. *That went well.*

12

It was still early morning and Bill had some time to kill. He grabbed a newspaper and stopped for breakfast. Sitting in the small restaurant drinking coffee, Bill began to think about how it seemed as if everything had fallen into place the last few days. Either this bubble of good luck was going to burst or this was payback for losing Amber. Having never gone to church, he wasn't sure if God worked this way or not. Then again, who knew if the bad guys would show up to get their money, or maybe the law would find out about what he had done. Either way he would lose, but he had a plan and was going to stick with it. Again, Bill thought about how people react after a lottery win. After winning millions of dollars, they end up penniless, in debt and hopelessly depressed.

Bill wasn't going to let that happen. He liked to think he was smarter than that.

The headline of the paper read 'Armored Truck Missing'. Bill read the article twice and from what he gathered the authorities had no idea where it was or what happened. Everybody was looking for it from the local police to the FBI and Bill thought *the crooks too*. One of the guards had been found in the forest but wasn't able to shed much light on the heist.

Bill wanted more information but the story didn't give a lot of detail, just a lot of filler. Names of the police spokesman, times and dates and unimportant stuff that nobody cared about. But it did say there weren't any suspects at this time.

"More coffee?" the waitress asked, snapping him back to reality.

"No thanks." He gave her a twenty and told her to keep the change. Bill had always wanted to be able to do that and now he could. As he got in his truck, Bill replayed step by step what he had done. He was sure he hadn't left a trace of anything to link him to the crime.

Driving back to Hendersonville, he stopped at a payphone and called Amber's sister, Amy. Amy and her husband traveled a lot and maybe she could recommend a travel agent. Well at least that was the excuse he used to call her.

After the pleasantries, she told him the name of a good company and who to see.

"You doing okay, Bill? We miss seeing you," Amy said in a soft but, sad voice.

"I'm doing okay, but I still miss your sister every day. What's worse are the things I know I should have said or done when she was around. Nights can be bad," Bill responded, trying his best not to sob.

"Time will help. It's always harder for those of us who are left behind, not the one who's gone."

Bill had never thought of it like that.

"Try not to be a stranger."

"It's hard seeing you all, but I'll try to stop by. I better go before I lose it. Bye." He hung up, trying to maintain his composure.

He sat in his truck as waves of depression washed over him. Bill looked up at the fall sky and thought, *I'd give all the money back if I could just be with her again. Even for one day.* He hung his head, knowing it was impossible and it took all his mental strength not to let the depression suck him down. Bill forced himself to start the truck and put it in gear. Pulling into traffic made him come back to life and concentrate on driving as he headed for the travel company.

13

Sitting in the jet high above the ground gave Bill a giddy feeling. It was early Thursday morning and he was going to be in Grand Cayman for lunch. He had flown several times before, but never first class. It was the only way to fly. He thought maybe it was too extravagant. Then again, maybe not.

The earlier part of the week went by in a flash. Scott and Fred had worked hard to help Bill make the little building nice enough to live in and Bill was able to work out all the details with Scott before he left. As soon as Bill got back into town, he would close on the property and then the real work would begin. By then, Scott should have the little building finished with electricity and a bathroom. Bill's only worry at this point was hoping the FedEx package arrived at the condo on time.

Just before he left, Bill had packaged up a small box of cash to ship to the condo in Grand Cayman where he was headed. When asked what it was, he told the fellow at the FedEx store it was tools. He told Bill it would be no problem to ship and that it would be delivered Friday morning. That was perfect. Bill was amazed at how much money you could get into a shoebox.

After gathering his luggage, Bill went through customs, which was pretty much a joke. The customs agent barely went through the dive bag that was full of Bill's worn out dive gear and a great deal of cash, hidden of course. Bill didn't look like he had much of anything, so the agent really had no reason to thoroughly search him.

"Welcome to Grand Cayman. Have a great stay and be safe diving," the customs agent told Bill as he stamped his passport. "Boy, that was easier than I thought," Bill mused. He grabbed a taxi that took him to his condo. Checking in at the office, the young girl was surprised Bill was alone.

The condo was nice – light and airy, a two story affair. Down stairs was a kitchen and living room with glass doors that opened to the beach. The second floor had one large bedroom with a small balcony. There was another small bedroom with a bath between the two. Bill retrieved a pair of shorts from his suitcase and went to the beach.

The condo was located on the opposite end of town on the Seven Mile Beach. In fact, a couple hundred yards past the condo complex, the beach narrowed to almost nothing. The complex wasn't big considering it only contained eight two-story condos. The weather was very hot and humid—a far cry from North Carolina's cool and dry air. Bill loved the weather although the ocean was the draw—going from crystal clear to a deep blue with shades of green in between.

Bill started walking up the beach and immediately began to feel better about things. This is what he needed, he was sure. R and R in the truest sense of the word. Every other vacation he had ever been on there was something to worry about, but not this time. Money was not a problem and now there was no job he had to get back to. Bill was comfortable with Scott finishing his "shed." The closing for the property was moving forward. There was certainly no way anyone could figure out that he, Bill August, got the money out of that truck, right?

Bill went over and over the details of that night searching for mistakes. He had worn gloves the entire time. The night was miserably dark and damp. No one was out, so no one saw him. He had been careful not to draw attention to himself by putting too much in his account. All the change was gone and now all Bill had to do was wait for the FedEx package to arrive.

The only thing that he wished was different was to have Amber with him. Amy's words echoed in his head, "Time will help. It's harder on the ones left behind." Bill's mind wandered. Maybe Earth was hell and the people who died were the lucky ones. He could feel a darkness overtaking him again and quickly shook it off.

Turning around he realized how far he had walked and he had to concentrate to get his bearings straight. There was a large, high-rise hotel to his left and the ocean on the right. Chairs were lined up in the white sand and young girls were serving cold drinks to people sitting under the umbrellas. Bill decided to go and sit down. A pretty waitress appeared.

"Would you like something to drink?" she asked.

Bill looked her up and down. "Sure, how about a bottled water with some ice."

"Be right back."

And she was right back. It was a good thing because Bill was almost asleep when she returned.

It was late when Bill awoke from his nap, but it was perfect timing. The sun was setting on the horizon and Bill watched it as it dipped below the ocean, half expecting to see steam appear. It was breathtakingly beautiful.

Man, I must have been tired, he thought as he looked around to gather his wits.

On his way back to the condo, Bill ate dinner at a local dive bar. Once he was in his room he tried to watch TV, but fell asleep again. Some jet-setting millionaire he was turning out to be.

The next morning someone knocking on the door startled Bill awake. *The maid maybe, not at a condo.* He trudged his way over to the door still half-asleep and to his pleasant surprise, it was the FedEx man with a package for him. Bill signed the clipboard and received his package. Thinking it was early for a delivery, Bill checked his watch. It was already 10:30. That's the latest he had slept in years. Actually, it was the best he had slept since 9/11. Bill showered and dressed.

Stepping out the door, the humidity hit him like a wall. He spotted a tall, thin, black man cleaning up around the shrubs. Bill noticed the man's small pickup with tools and debris in the back of it.

The man glistened with sweat, so Bill went back in and fixed a large glass of ice and grabbed a bottle of water from the fridge.

"Here you go, partner. It looks like you could use this."

The black man turned and cocked his head at Bill like a dog that had just heard a strange noise. The man wrapped his long, bony fingers around the glass and Bill filled it up. He took a long drink of the refreshing water.

"I sure do appreciate that, mister."

"No problem," Bill answered.

The young girl from the office opened the glass door and looked at Bill and the black man.

"Is there a problem?" she asked. Her voice was too sweet and as she stood in the doorway she fanned her hand in front of her face.

"Not unless you got one," Bill yelled back.

This was not the answer she expected. Pinching her face up, she shut the door and went back to her air conditioning.

"What a bitch," Bill muttered under his breath.

The black man stuck out his hand and proceeded, "Thanks again. My name is Jonas."

Bill had to concentrate on every word the man said. His accent was a mixture of British and Black Caribbean.

"Do you work for her?" Bill asked, thinking he might have jeopardized his job.

"No, I work for myself," Jonas replied proudly.

"Well, don't work too hard." And Bill turned to go, then turned back.

"Maybe you can help me out."

"How's that?" Jonas was curious.

"I'm not from around here, like that's hard to tell," Bill said sarcastically. "Anyway, I want to do some fishing. I wonder if you can suggest a boat or captain."

"Sure, mister. Let me finish here. I will take you myself."

"Name's Bill and no mister."

Bill went back to his condo to get some stuff. He crammed a small backpack with essentials: suntan lotion, extra sunglasses, a towel and, oh yes, cash.

Jonas' truck was cramped with the two men almost rubbing shoulders. The dash was covered with paper and sticky notes.

"That's my office," Jonas laughed.

"If it works for you, it works for me," was all Bill said as he took in all around him.

It's one thing to be on the main road in a taxi. It was quite another to be driving around with a local. Bill liked it.

Within ten minutes, they were at a small boat dock on the other side of the island. It wasn't fancy and Bill could see that it was a working boat dock, not a fancy charter boat or yacht dock. There were several sport fishing boats tied up at the slips, but no big pleasure boats or sails.

Everybody waved or said hey to Jonas as he and Bill walked up the dock. They reached a boated named "Grand Illusion," and Jonas jumped aboard. It was a modest fishing boat that looked as if it was spotlessly clean and in very good condition. Jonas knocked on the cabin door and an old fellow with a grey beard and white captain's hat appeared.

"Good morning, Jonas. How you doing?" the Captain asked.

"Good, good, Captain. This man wants to fish. Wahoo, dolphin, maybe a marlin," Jonas informed the Captain, motioning towards Bill.

The Captain sized up Bill and asked, "Ever been out fishing before, young fellow?" *Everybody's young compared to this old salt*, Bill thought.

"No sir," admitted Bill in his North Carolina drawl. The old Captain looked like someone you said "sir" to. The two men continued to look each other over.

The Captain was barefooted, barrel-chested and wore the captain's hat back on his head and white shorts that hung to his knees. He could pass for Hemingway's twin.

The Captain saw Bill as a tourist, but at least he was respectful.

"Well, fishing has been slow, but it still beats baking on the beach. Half day or whole?"

"Whole day," Bill answered.

"Be here at six tomorrow. I'll supply tackle, bait, sandwiches and drinks. If you need anything else, you bring it. It'll be $500, no checks or cards."

That left only cash and he had plenty.

"No problem. I'll see you in the morning."

The Captain turned to Jonas. "You want to mate?"

"Yes, Captain," and Jonas nodded towards Bill. The Captain got the gesture.

"Good," the Captain said as he turned to Bill again. "Best damn mate on the island and he'd rather trim bushes. Name's James, but everybody calls me Captain." The Captain stuck out his hand to Bill and they shook. Bill thought, *everybody ought to call you Ernie.*

With the deal struck, Bill and Jonas got back in the truck.

"Thanks, man. I would never have found this place. Go by a gas station so I can put some gas in your truck," Bill said to Jonas, trying not to sound bossy.

"You don't have to do that Mister Bill."

"I know, but with the price of gas here and you running me around, shoot, that's the least I could do. One more thing. You could drop me off in town. I need to go to the bank."

"Sure thing, Mister Bill."

"Just Bill, please."

"Ah, okay Mis…uh, Bill." Both Jonas and Bill laughed out loud.

As Bill got out of the truck at the bank, Jonas inquired, "How you getting' home, man?"

"I'll walk. I could use the exercise. Do you think you could pick me up in the morning?"

"Be ready by five. Captain don't like being late." Jonas drove off.

Bill went into the bank and opened up an account. He made the minimum deposit to start a checking account. Stopping at two more banks, he did the same thing. Bill kept a small notebook which he wrote everything in: the name of the bank, the amount and date of deposits and of course, a total. Bill decided six accounts were enough, three here in the Caymans and three at home. He planned to make deposits every day while on vacation.

***

Bill was waiting outside when Jonas pulled into the condo parking lot.

"I hope you drink coffee, Jonas," Bill said as he thrust a cup in the window.

"Thank you and good morning, Mis…I mean Bill."

"You're going to have to stop that crap." They both laughed again.

Once at the dock, both Jonas and Captain went to work and left Bill on the dock feeling like a third wheel. When the three of them got far enough out on the water, Jonas got all the lines baited and in the sea. The Captain stayed on the flying bridge scanning for fish while he trolled up and down a weed line. Bill was sitting in the fighting chair, totally relaxed and almost asleep when the first fish hit.

After that, the fish really started biting. Bill caught dolphin and wahoo all morning long and he was having the time of his life. Jonas was an expert mate, telling Bill when and how to work the rod and reel. Every now and then, the Captain would yell down some command and Jonas would comply. Bill couldn't make out what was being said between the engine noise and the accent.

"What are you doing?" Bill asked Jonas as he began to bring in the tackle and stow the rods.

"Captain's going to a different spot, after the big fish."

Big fish, Bill thought. *Hell, these are big fish, the biggest I've ever caught!* Up to now, the biggest fish he had ever caught were blues at Cape Hatteras. Every October, Bill would meet some friends at the Cape to fish for a couple of days and just hang out when the blues were running. It was a good time—a time Bill would never forget and he regretted that they hadn't done it in a long time and eventually drifted apart. That was a lifetime ago or so it seemed.

Bill realized he was daydreaming again when the reel on the left side started to scream. After Jonas grabbed the pole and set it between Bill's legs, he scooped up some sea water in a small bucket.

"Pull back, Mister Bill! Pull back hard!" Jonas yelled as he poured the water on the reel. It started to steam.

"Every time you pull back, try and crank the reel as you go forward," Jonas yelled again.

Things were happening fast and just like that, a beautiful, dark blue marlin leapt out of the water about 100 yards behind the boat. The fish looked as if it froze in midair before falling back into the sea. All three men let out a yell. At that second Bill thought, *Life doesn't get much better than this.*

Bill pulled back hard, bracing his legs against the bottom of the fighting chair. This was a difficult task and the sweat was running down his face and back. Bill fought the fish for the better part of two hours. When he finally got it close to the boat, he realized how tired he was. Everybody was tired, but Bill and the fish were exhausted. As Bill looked over the side of the boat where Jonas held the big fish by the bill and leader, he couldn't help but admire its beauty and strength. Bill turned to Jonas. "Cut it loose."

"But Bill…"

"Cut it loose, Jonas. I won. That's enough for me."

Jonas worked the hook from the marlin's mouth, held him for a moment and let him swim free. The Captain looked at Bill and nodded. Nothing needed to be said, but the Captain gained a new respect for the man from North Carolina.

They fished the rest of the day but didn't catch much. Bill didn't care if the hooks were even baited. He was exhausted.

They got back to the dock around 6:00 and Jonas threw the fish they had caught from the well to the dock. He and the Captain cleaned the boat and stowed the gear. A small crowd gathered to see the catch as Jonas jumped onto the dock and began to clean the fish. Bill paid the Captain.

"That marlin was over 400 pounds. It would have made a helluva trophy," the captain told Bill.

"Maybe so, but he's better off out there than on my wall."

"Any time you wanna go out, just call me. I like the way you fish." The Captain and Bill shook hands. "Not bad for a tourist. Not bad at all."

Jonas was still cleaning fish as Bill and the Captain stepped off the boat.

"I can't take all that meat, Captain. It'll go bad," Bill explained.

"Take what you want. I'll give some of it away and sell the rest," the Captain told Bill.

"What you sell, does that come off my bill?" Bill asked.

The Captain looked at Bill and grinned. "Not hardly," and they laughed.

Someone in the crowd of people remarked to Jonas about the number of fish that had been caught.

"You should have seen the one we let go," Jonas gloated without looking up from his task.

"Well, if that don't sound like a fish story, nothing does," remarked another dockside tourist.

"He's not kidding. Bill here fought that marlin for two hours or better before bringing it up to the boat," the Captain told the group. Bill rubbed his butt. He had the bruises to prove it.

"Why did you let it go, Captain?" asked a small boy.

"I didn't, Bill did. It was his catch."

Bill looked at the boy and responded, "So you can catch it when you get a little bigger."

Everybody in the group chuckled.

Jonas drove Bill back to the condo. Bill was bone tired and every muscle and bone in his body ached. He handed Jonas $300.

"That's too much, Bill."

"Look, that was and will be, one of the highlights of my life. Take it; you earned it. See you around," and Bill got out of the truck. He grabbed his cooler of fish and headed for his door as Jonas drove away. All Bill could think about was his bed.

14

Bill slept in the next morning. After showering, he looked in the mirror and noticed that his face was brown except for where his sunglasses protected his eyes. He looked at his arms and legs and saw that they were dark brown too. He laughed when he realized he was starting to look like a native after only three days. Bill called Scott to see how things were going on the mountain. He wanted to make sure he had a place to stay when he got back to Hendersonville.

Scott told him they would be finished tomorrow. "We finished insulating and paneling the walls. All the plumbing is finished and the flooring is down. It's small, but livable." The septic and electrical would be tied in tomorrow. The electric company had set a temporary pole and meter for construction. Scott would wire the shed to it for power.

"Thanks for the help, man. I'll see you when I get home this weekend." Bill was excited about the progress that had been made.

There was a knock on the door and Bill told Scott he had to go. Jonas was on the other side of the door with two young boys by his side.

"Bill."

"Jonas."

"My wife is cooking some of the fish you caught for dinner. I would like you to join my family and me. If you like, I'll pick you up at six okay man?"

It took Bill by surprise. He looked down at the boys. "What do you think, fellows?" Their dress was sparse—sandals and shorts.

"Mister, you'd be a fool to miss my mama's cookin'. Besides, we be havin' all the family."

"Well, I can't miss Mama's cooking."

"Thank you, Bill. See you at six."

"No, Jonas. Thank you. Do I need to bring anything?"

Jonas smiled, his teeth brilliantly white against his dark black face.

"Just come hungry, because my wife is the best cook on the island."

Jonas turned to leave. "Thanks again," Bill said as he watched the boys pile into the truck.

I sure didn't see that coming, Bill thought.

Bill got dressed, stuffed a paper bag full of money and left for Georgetown. He did his banking and decided to wander around town. It was a clean, small port town. Bill checked out the different shops, bought a few tee shirts and started back to the beach. Walking by a jewelry store, Bill couldn't help but look in the window. On display were several watches, one of which caught his eye. Bill had carefully studied the watch for several minutes when he finally realized it was a Rolex. A black lady inside noticed that Bill had been standing there for a while and opened the door.

"Come inside and you can get a better look."

"No. No thank you, ma'am. I might end up buying it."

"Come on in, man. It won't hurt to look at it."

Bill left the shop with the stainless and black Rolex on his wrist. *What a sucker,* he thought, as he felt the watch heavy around his wrist.

He was looking at his reflection in the face of his watch thinking about how nice it would be to have Amber by his side when, just as promised, Jonas' truck pulled into the condo parking lot at 6:00. Jonas was prompt. Bill did a double take when the truck pulled to a stop where he was waiting. He had been expecting Jonas, but behind the wheel sat a beautiful young girl. After staring at her for what felt like an eternity, he gathered his wits and said, "You're not Jonas."

That was a brilliant statement, you idiot. Of course she wasn't. And she was beautiful. Her skin was lighter than Bill's and her head was covered with curly hair that was mostly black with some brown streaks. Her large, dark eyes sparkled as she smiled. Bill couldn't get over how gorgeous she was and almost lost his balance as she spoke.

"I'm Victoria. Jonas is my dad. He's helping my mom with dinner. I'm here to pick you up." Her voice was soft, with a little island dialect. Bill was at a loss for words. His mind had lost control of his mouth and body. He couldn't move and he was afraid to say anything for fear of something stupid coming out. Again.

Their eyes locked together and neither wanted to look away. Finally, Bill shook his head and said, "I got something for your dad." Bill pulled out a bottle of Cayman rum from a bag.

Still holding eye contact, Victoria frowned a little and politely said, "Two years ago he would have loved that, but he stopped drinking when he became a Christian."

Bill shook his head in disbelief. *How many more surprises am I in for tonight? A Christian*, Bill thought. *I can't believe that. I thought I left the Bible Belt. Maybe this is the Bible Belt of the Caribbean.*

Bill couldn't bear to take his eyes off Victoria as he deposited the rum in a nearby trashcan. He felt like a little boy staring at a new toy and he just couldn't break free. He just knew she must have considered him childish for the way he was acting.

It only got worse as he sat in the confines of the small truck. All of Bill's hair seemed to tingle and stand on end. He was afraid to say anything for fear of embarrassing himself more than he already had. He remembered the old adage about staying quiet and letting people think you're an idiot rather than speaking and removing all doubt.

Victoria wasn't immune to what was happening. She used all her strength to pull her eyes from Bill's and slip the truck into gear. She didn't want the moment to end as she drove back to her home as slowly as possible.

Jonas waved as the truck pulled into the drive. At first, poor Jonas thought something was wrong. It had taken Victoria a long time to get back and now no one was getting out of the truck. He finally walked to the truck and looked in to make sure everything was alright. He knew right away what was going on, even if the occupants didn't want to admit it to him. Bill and Victoria were staring at each other again, but this time with silly grins on their faces.

"What's so funny?" Jonas asked.

"Nothing, Daddy."

Bill looked around, *when did we get here?*

"Your mom needs some help, Vic."

Victoria looked at Bill before she got out of the truck and said something that Jonas couldn't hear. "I wish the drive could have been longer."

"That's my oldest," Jonas told Bill.

"She must take after her mother 'cause she's more enjoyable to look at than you."

Both men laughed.

"Come on. Let me show you the rest of my family."

Bill didn't meet just the children. He met aunts, uncles, cousins, second cousins and Jonas' mother. She looked like she must have been a hundred years old. Her hair was as white as snow and her skin looked and probably felt like old shoe leather. It was obvious she spent her life in the sun.

After Jonas introduced Bill to the matriarch, she motioned him closer. Bill bent down to the old woman and she put a bony arm around his head and put her lips to his ear.

"Welcome to the family," she said, flashing a sly smile. Bill pulled away slowly, not sure what to make of the old woman's comment.

A long dinner table made of plywood and sawhorses had been set up in the yard. There were kitchen chairs, beach chairs, boxes and buckets to sit on as a crowd gathered. Everybody was chatting and smiling and the smell of dinner hung in the air. Jonas sat at the head of the table and motioned Bill to a chair next to him.

Bill couldn't help but notice that he was the only white person present, but no one else noticed or seemed to care. He felt as if he stood out like a sore thumb even with the number of people there. The only person with lighter skin was Victoria and that was only because of Bill's tan.

Soon everyone had found a seat at the table and Jonas motioned for everyone to stand and yelled, "Hurry, Ma Ma. We're going to say the blessing."

A slender, middle-aged woman came out the front door. Her skin glistened with perspiration as she fanned her blouse to cool off. Victoria did take after her mother. "You must be Bill. I am Elizabeth. I sure have heard a great deal about you lately. Between Jonas and Victoria I was expecting someone…bigger," she said, smiling at Bill.

"Now Ma Ma, behave," Jonas said.

Bill blushed red, completely embarrassed.

"Nice to meet you," was all Bill could mutter.

Everyone stood as Jonas said the blessing. Several women followed Elizabeth into the house to retrieve the food and the feast was on.

Bill fielded questions from everyone, except the person he really wanted to converse with—Victoria. She just picked at her food and glanced at Bill from time to time.

"So, where ya' from, Bill?" asked Elizabeth.

"North Carolina, the western part. In the mountains."

Someone asked if it ever snowed there.

"Sometimes, but the winters are mostly mild."

One of the children said he had never seen real snow except in pictures and movies.

"Do you like Grand Cayman?"

"I love it. It's beautiful, but expensive."

"You should live here," Jonas remarked.

"Well, that's funny you should say that. I'm thinking about buying the condo I'm staying at."

"Would you lease it or rent it when you're not here?" Jonas asked.

"No, I don't think so. I'm kinda funny about things like that. I want to be able to come and go anytime I please. Besides, that would be rough on the place. Nobody takes good care of things anymore."

"I know what you mean. I've been fishing with the Captain long enough to realize that people abuse everything. They have even lost reels and rods overboard. It can get nasty." Jonas continued, "You must have a very good job to be able to afford the condo and take off when you want."

"Actually, I just got fired and this trip was my reward to myself."

Bill could see confusion on Jonas' face. Bill smiled and explained. He hated to lie to Jonas, but the inheritance story seemed to be the best explanation and in a way the money was an inheritance… Right?

They ate and conversed for about an hour or so. Fish, rice and beans with plenty of hot sauce. Bill wasn't used to this much spice and his mouth was on fire. People started getting up from the table and taking their dishes inside, but Jonas and Bill stayed talking at the table. Bill quizzed Jonas about fishing and the fishing boat and asked him why he didn't Captain his own.

"Several years back I was a drinking man," Jonas explained. "Because of that, I almost lost everything. One night after passing out on the side of the road, a young man with a bunch of teenagers picked me up. They helped me home and to make a long story short, they were a church group from the States. They came by the next day to see if I was okay. No one pressured or interrogated me, but they kept mentioning their walk with God and what he had done for them. One thing led to another and God moved in my life. I got saved right then and there. I started attending church and, I promise it's been the greatest event in my life. I don't drink, try not to cuss and I see God's work in my life every day. Life can't get much better than this."

Bill had to agree that everything had been great tonight. In fact, every time he was around Jonas he could feel peace radiating out from him. There were no bad feelings here tonight and Jonas' family accepted Bill as if they had known him for years. Something good had invaded this place and these people.

Jonas and Bill sat and talked for a little while longer before Jonas got up to help in the kitchen. Bill rose with Jonas with the intention of lending a helping hand.

"No man, you're my guest. Please just sit."

"But Jonas, I feel guilty doing nothing," Bill protested.

"Just sit."

Just then, Bill spied Victoria. Jonas collected some dishes. "Vic, come keep our guest company."

He didn't have to say it twice. She came right over and sat down in her dad's seat.

At first they sat and looked at each other as Jonas continued to collect dishes. When he left for the kitchen, Bill knew he had to say something.

"You're the most beautiful woman I've ever seen." Victoria blushed and looked away. *Ah, what are you doing? That didn't come out right.*

"Thank you," Victoria whispered.

"I'm sorry. I didn't mean to embarrass you. It's just when you showed up to get me I was expecting your father and you caught me off guard. I couldn't regain my composure. I felt something; I still do. I just can't figure out what's happening. Does that sound stupid?"

Victoria reached across the table and grabbed Bill's hand.

"Well, at least you're honest. I felt it, too, if that helps any," she said as she gently squeezed Bill's hand.

Sitting there holding hands with this young girl, Bill's mind began to race. *What's happening here? Honestly, if she only knew. What about Amber? I can't believe I feel this way about someone after just meeting her.*

I can't let this happen. It's already happening. Oh, the hell with it. Let it happen. It feels great again.

Slowly, they began talking back and forth until the dam burst. Then each one was asking and answering questions, back and forth, back and forth. They sounded like a couple of birds singing to each other.

Bill glanced at his new watch and did a double take. Looking around, Bill realized that they were the only ones left. The house was quiet. Everyone had departed. When did that happen?

Jonas stepped out the front door and began taking down the lights strung across the yard. Bill and Victoria looked at each other and laughed.

"Jonas, I better get going. It's getting late," Bill called out.

"It is getting late. I couldn't stop you all from talking. It's the most I've seen my Victoria smile in a long time."

Victoria frowned. She didn't want Bill to leave and her dad's last statement embarrassed her.

"Vic, do you still have my keys? I'm sure you won't mind driving Bill home."

"Yes and no, Dad."

Jonas knew that tone. "Come right home. It's late."

The drive to the condo was silent, each lost in thought.

"Good night Victoria. Please be careful driving home." Bill got out of the truck.

"Good night Bill. I had a wonderful time tonight, but I think you forgot something," Victoria told Bill.

Victoria could tell by the look on Bill's face he hadn't a clue what she was talking about. With the truck still running, Victoria set the parking brake and got out. She walked to Bill and took both his hands in hers.

"A kiss," and she pressed her lips to his. Bill started to lose his balance and his world began to spin as soon as their lips pressed against each other. He had to embrace her to keep from falling over. It was over too soon and she was got back in the truck. She drove off, leaving Bill standing in the parking lot not knowing what to think. He never expected that. She tasted wonderful. *I'm sure not going to brush my teeth tonight*, he laughed to himself.

15

The next morning Bill awoke to the sound of a leaf blower. Looking out his window, he could see Jonas finishing up the yard work. Bill rushed to get dressed but took a moment to remember last night. He flew out the door, not wanting to miss Jonas.

"Hey Jonas, can I talk to you a minute?" Bill asked.

Jonas shut off the machine. "That's better mon. What didja say now?"

"I wanted to ask you something."

"What's on your mind?" Jonas asked, "another fishing trip".

"Well for starters, thanks for last night. The food and your family were great. It's the best time I've had in a long time." Since 9/10, Bill thought, but didn't mention it.

"But and it's a big but, I was wondering about Victoria." Jonas frowned a little. "I was wondering if I could take her to dinner or something." *Or something. What are you, an idiot? Or something. What was that supposed to mean?* "I mean a date or movie. I didn't mean…"

Jonas saw that Bill was struggling.

Bill felt a little awkward asking permission from a father for a date. After all, Bill was 34 years old and Victoria was 22, both adults, but he respected Jonas.

"Calm down, Bill. I know what you meant. Could we talk a little first?"

"Sure. Let's sit in the shade."

They walked to the back of the condo and sat at a picnic table facing each other. Bill felt nervous and fidgety. Jonas was surprised and had been caught off guard.

"Victoria is my firstborn and very special to me. I'm not blind. I can see how pretty she is and I know how smart she is even though she didn't go to college. She would have gone if I could have afforded it." Jonas paused. This next part was hard for him. "She has been in love before, but the guy was trouble. I wasn't sober enough to do anything to help her out. I feel like I let her down. Anyway, I saw how you two looked at each other and acted last night. I guess I was hoping that nothing would come of it. You know, the head in the sand thing." Jonas looked out across the ocean and continued. "You're going to be leaving in a few days and maybe never coming back. Where will that leave Victoria?"

Now it was Bill's turn. "Jonas, I understand your concern. I'm sure I'll be the same way one day. But and that's a huge but, I give you my word that my intentions are completely honest and up front. I want to date Victoria very much. I'm not married and I don't have someone waiting for me at home. I plan on living here at least part of the year every year." The whole time Bill spoke, he maintained eye contact with Jonas. "Look Jonas, I've made mistakes in the past. Everybody has. I don't know what will happen next in life any more than anyone else. I just know life is short and can get snatched away in the blink of an eye. Right now I'm at a crossroad and I feel as if I've been guided here. I just want a chance to prove that I'm what I say I am." Bill stopped. He didn't know if what he was saying made any sense to Jonas or not.

Jonas thought, *Lord help me. I don't know what to do.* He listened hard, hoping for an answer. It was hard on Jonas knowing that he wasn't there for his baby girl last time and she ended up hurt, yet she still loved and trusted him as her father. Victoria had seen the change in him after he stopped drinking. She was the first in the family to attend church with him and was even the first to accept Christ. She was very special and he wouldn't let her down again.

"Bill, I don't want you to take this wrong. I like you, really. The only way she can go out with you is if Elizabeth and I come along."

Bill thought for a moment. "What the heck, no problem. As long as you let me pick the restaurant and pay the bill, no questions asked."

Jonas started to say something.

"No questions asked," Bill repeated.

Jonas looked at Bill and smiled. "Ok then. I'll tell Elizabeth."

"Good then, it's settled. I'll pick you up at six this evening."

"Aren't you forgetting something?" Bill looked confused. "You better ask Victoria. She may have other plans." Jonas could see the wind leave Bill's sails. "Don't worry. She doesn't, but you better get a move on. Vic only gets a half hour for lunch."

Bill parked his newly rented car in front of the largest basin at the turtle farm. That's what the locals called it. Officially, it was the Turtle Research Station. Looking around, he spotted Victoria eating a bagged lunch with some other ladies. As Bill walked to the covered tables, Victoria looked up and smiled as she recognized Bill. She bounced up and met him halfway. Without the slightest hesitation, she kissed him. Again, she had caught him off guard.

"Would you like to go to dinner with me tonight?" he blurted out.

She was cautious about answering.

"I've already spoken to your dad and he and your mom would like to come."

He didn't tell her it wasn't an option.

A smile spread across her face. "Yes, yes I think it'll be great."

"Good. I'll pick you up at six."

She grabbed his hand as Bill began to turn away and pulled him back. She stood on her toes and leaned into him. Her lips brushed his cheek with the lightest kiss Bill had ever felt. In an instant, she was gone. His hand went to his cheek as he looked after her. *I have to leave in two days. That won't be fun, but I'm sure tonight will be,* he thought.

Bill was early. He just couldn't wait to see Victoria again. Time was running out and he wanted to spend all of it with her. When making the reservations, Bill requested a table on the outside balcony. They had a nice view of the ocean and the streets of the small city. With a light ocean breeze and the setting sun everyone settled into their chairs comfortably. The conversation started slowly, but, in no time at all, the four of them could hardly stop speaking long enough to order food. They talked about everything: Bill's life to this point, money, or the lack of it in Jonas' case. There was no tension of any kind between Jonas and Bill. It helped that Jonas and he had been developing a friendship. Dinner was perfect. The food and service were good.

The only awkward moment came when Bill started to eat before Jonas said the blessing. Bill apologized and they all bowed their heads. Jonas asked the Lord to bless the food and thanked Him for the family's many blessings. Then he thanked Him for Bill's friendship and asked God to show Bill all His great works. They all said, "Amen," including Bill.

Bill thanked Jonas for praying. No one had mentioned him in a prayer before—at least while he was present. Jonas went into a long explanation about the power of prayer, but before he could get too far along, Elizabeth put her hand on Jonas' arm and smiled at him, reminding him not to preach an entire sermon.

"Sometimes he gets so excited about God, he can't hold it in," Elizabeth told Bill.

"At home, we call people like him preachers," Bill said.

Jonas beamed at that statement.

It was time to order dessert and Bill realized time was running out with his new friends. Bill thought about it: "new friends." He didn't have many old friends. It was strange how comfortable he felt around these people in such a short amount time. The waitress appeared and set a glass of dark amber liquid down in front of Jonas.

"Compliments of Pop Pop," she said, smiled and walked away.

Jonas just stared at the glass. Elizabeth and Victoria looked at each other in horror. Bill could tell something was wrong.

"Who's Pop Pop?" Bill asked.

Jonas looked at Victoria and nodded.

"It's only fair, honey. He'll find out sooner or later," Jonas told her.

"Ok," Victoria's voice was almost a whisper. She looked directly into Bill's eyes and began to speak.

"I dated Bobby all through high school. I was head over heels in love with him, but he was in love with money and drugs. At first I didn't know, and when I started to realize it, I just decided to turn a blind eye. As time went on, things got worse and worse. He pulled me into his world of disaster. Daddy was drinking heavily and couldn't do anything about the situation and Mom was doing everything she could just to hold the family together." She paused and bit her lip. "One night Bobby and I had a terrible fight. He hit me and I left. Everybody was high, including me. I had to get loose or he might hurt me badly..." She paused and looked as if she was pushing painful memories out of her mind. "I staggered onto the beach and, fortunately, a group of young people from the same church that witnessed to Daddy found me. They didn't press me or anything; they just wanted to help me home. We were walking along the street when Bobby and a carload of guys came by. I was leaning on one boy who was holding me up when I noticed the car turn around. At first I thought they were going to run us over, but then I heard the gunshots." Victoria put her head down. "The bullets struck the young man helping me. It didn't kill him, but it paralyzed him. He's confined to a wheelchair because of me. It's my fault." She began to weep. Bill put his arm around her and offered a napkin. Victoria continued, "From then on Bobby told me anybody who dated me would end up the same way……. or worse"

"Was he arrested?"

"The cops caught him and the rest of his crew. He went to jail, but he'll be getting out soon."

Jonas was still looking at the glass. Bill reached across the table, grabbed the glass and drank it. Cayman rum surely tasted good.

Wiping his mouth Bill asked, "So tell me. Who is Pop Pop?"

Everybody at the table looked at each other. Jonas spoke first. "After the shooting, all of Bobby's buddies started calling him Pop Pop, because that's the sound his gun made that night."

"Must not have been much of a gun," Bill commented.

Jonas didn't know how to take Bill's last comment. The table was quiet as they looked back and forth at each other. The silence was heavy when a thin, young, black man with long dreadlocks appeared. He eyed the empty glass.

"Did you enjoy that rum as before, Jonas?" the black boy asked.

"He didn't, but I sure did, " Bill answered, "how bout another?"

"And who are you, white boy?"

"I'm Jonas' friend and I can tell you're not. So why not move along before you get hurt," Bill threatened in a low, hushed tone.

"Jonas, you better tell your white friend here to respect Pop Pop's posse."

"Pop Pop being the coward who shoots unarmed people," Bill said before Jonas could answer.

Jonas' eyes got as big as silver dollars.

"Pop Pop will be outa jail in three weeks and he'll deal with you. And you too, Victoria."

"Tell him to bring something bigger than a pop gun, 'cause he's gonna need it. And in the meantime, if anything and I mean anything, happens to my friends here, not only will he not have a posse to come back to, but he won't have a family either," Bill hissed. "That means you will be number one, Rasta boy," and Bill began to get out of his seat. His fingers slid into his pants pocket and wrapped around a knife. Bill couldn't believe what he was doing. He had never spoken like that or threatened anyone in his life. He never had the need, but he wasn't going to let anything happen to this family.

The dreadlocked boy took several steps back. He wasn't prepared for someone to stand up to him. No one on the island carried a weapon, not even the police and here this man was reaching for something.

Bill pulled the knife and it flashed open as he lunged for the young man. Bill pressed it under the man's chin and said, "Do we understand each other?" The tone and sound of Bill's voice scared the Rastafarian more than the knife. "Tell Pop Pop I won't be hard to find. I'll be with Victoria."

With that said, Bill let go of the dark fellow and pushed him away. The young man didn't expect or want this kind of trouble and ran off.

Bill stood shaking until Victoria put her arm through his and kissed his cheek. "Thank you."

The drive back to Jonas' house was quiet. Jonas invited Bill in for the coffee and dessert they never got at the restaurant. Elizabeth broke the tension by saying she never saw a black boy look as white as she had this evening. Everyone laughed and they went inside. Bill stayed late and he and Victoria went on the back porch overlooking the docks.

**

Victoria took off work to spend the whole next day with Bill. They laid on the beach until noon, then drove to the far end of the island where they had lunch and rented jet skis. Both thought life couldn't get any better, but Bill couldn't forget that he was leaving soon.

At lunch, Bill learned that Jonas worked hard to keep his head above water. Jonas couldn't get a regular job because most everybody knew about his past drinking problem. He had burned a lot of bridges before drying out. Working for himself was Jonas' only option, except the occasional fishing trip. The Captain used Jonas as a mate on every trip out. He was the only person to stand by Jonas even when he was drinking. Some friends you can't even beat off with a stick. The Captain told Jonas time and time again he should try and get another boat, but he couldn't afford it.

Victoria told Bill it wasn't uncommon to have bill collectors call the house, but she was always sure that God would provide. Bill couldn't understand her faith. He thought that he was in control of his own life and didn't know how to depend on someone or something he couldn't even see.

Bill looked at Victoria lying on the white, sandy beach. She was stunning. Her beauty was breathtaking. In Bill's eyes, everything about her was perfect, her skin and her hair. Everything. As she lay there, Bill traced her arm. The electricity was definitely still there. He had never felt such a connection before. At his touch, Victoria sat up and Bill knew he had to try and explain his feelings.

"Victoria, I'm not much on the sappy stuff, but I don't want to leave. I don't know what to do or feel. You've got me running in circles. It's gotten so I can't think straight. In my eyes, you're perfect. You first reeled me in by your natural beauty, but now I can see that there is so much more to you."

She smiled at him and her dark eyes sparkled like the sun on the water.

"God knows what he's doing, Bill. He put you in my family's life for a reason. I have actually been praying God would put someone like you in my life. The night I picked you up I knew those prayers had been answered. Granted, we've only known each other for a few days, but the feeling is overwhelming. This is hard to say, but I am in love with you…"

Bill couldn't believe it. Victoria used the "L" word. She wasn't shy about her feelings. *What do I say?*

"What are we going to do? I mean, yes, I feel it too. It's just that…I can't use my words," and Bill pulled her to him. They didn't kiss, but he held her, hoping she understood what he was trying to say.

There they sat for the rest of the day, making plans and committing themselves to each other. That evening eating dinner with the family, there was a calm between Victoria and Bill. Jonas and Elizabeth both noticed and already knew what was going on between them.

The next morning before going to the airport, Bill went to the banks to make one last deposit. What a trip! A whirlwind. He caught a huge fish, met some great people, fell in love, started three bank accounts and bought a Rolex and a condo on the beach. What else could happen? Then it hit him. Bill went to the bank officer who helped him open his account.

"I can't give you that kind of information," the assistant manager told Bill in a very British accent.

"I'm pretty sure he does, because I overheard him say something about this bank. I want to deposit money in his account." When Bill said that the man looked up. Bill knew he had his attention. "Could you please help me out?"

The assistant manager thought for a minute. "This is highly out of the ordinary. If I can even do this, how much would you like to deposit?" The banker knew Jonas had an account, because the two of them had spoken several times. His and Elizabeth's account was shaky, at best.

"$10,000 US," Bill answered, very nonchalantly.

The banker's eyes lit up. This was an opportunity not to be missed. Now Jonas' account wouldn't be so shaky and he could pay the bank the money that he owed them. Besides, why should the bank care where the money came from? Bill was playing with the banker's natural mentality and money, cash money, was a big factor.

"Ok, I'll do it. Just this once."

"You'll not regret this, I promise," Bill said, looking at the nameplate on the desk. "Mr. Binge, thank you."

Jonas and Victoria were at the airport to see Bill off. Jonas shook Bill's hand then embraced him. Bill turned to Victoria and lifted her chin with his hand. "You promised no tears," he said. "I'll be back in three weeks."

She shook her head and said, "Kiss me, please."

Bill gave her a small kiss on the lips. It was hard, knowing Jonas was standing nearby.

"No, I mean kiss me. Like the first time."

They embraced and kissed. The room swirled and neither wanted to let go and then Bill was gone.

16

As Bill sat in the jet, his thoughts wandered. He had deposited just under $200,000 in Cayman banks over the course of several days. Not bad. What a cheapskate he was for only giving Jonas ten grand! And Victoria. That kiss in the airport? He could still taste her. Maybe that would last three weeks, maybe not. *What does Jonas think?* Bill couldn't keep his eyes open any longer.

The steward woke him as they landed in Atlanta. As he rushed through the crowd in the airport, he remembered why he hated it there. His friends back home would say that you have to go through the Atlanta airport to get to hell—it was always jam packed with people. Bill changed planes for the short trip to Asheville. Although it felt good to be home, he could feel the pressure of his actions as he went about his business at the airport.

On his way to the mountain retreat, Bill stopped in the Verizon store to purchase a cell phone. For something that seemed like it would be easy to set up, it took forever, but was worth the wait. At least now he could call Victoria. Bill was already longing for her and he could still taste her kiss.

Bill was very self-conscious about using the phone, mostly because it was new to him.

Everyone else seemed as if they had been born to talk on a cell phone. Even when he stopped to get groceries, people in the store were talking on the devices. What could be so important that they had to tell someone while shopping? Bill couldn't figure it out. What did people do before cell phones?

By the time Bill turned onto the dirt road on the way to his property, it was starting to get dark. He unlocked the chain that was hanging across the driveway and parked his truck. The key for the small storage building was right where he and Scott had agreed to leave it.

Entering the building, Bill was amazed at the transformation. Hardwood flooring with a small area rug, futon, paneled walls, TV, bar and cabinets with a sink, fridge and microwave. It was hard to believe how it looked when Scott started out. The bathroom was just as perfect. Bill had drawn the layout for Scott but hadn't expected this level of comfort and craftsmanship.

Bill put up the groceries and unpacked. The controls for the TV and DVD player lay on a small end table. There was going to be no problem living here. Small but cozy. He called Scott.

"Hey Scott. This is Bill."

"Hey Bill. This is Scott."

"You did a fantastic job up here. I just got back and I can't believe it! It's just…I can't believe it!"

"You may not believe the bill either." Scott laughed. "Just kidding. It went a little over, but it's close to what we figured."

"I want to catch up with you tomorrow to settle up and make plans to start the house. Would around ten be good with you?"

"Nuh uh. Tomorrow's Sunday. I'll be in church 'till lunch time. Hey, why don't you come and we can all go to eat afterwards. You can meet the family and all that crap. We could talk at lunch."

Bill thought for a moment. Church. Maybe someone's trying to tell him something. Jonas, Victoria and now Scott…

"You know what, Scott? That sounds like a good idea." Bill couldn't believe what he was agreeing to. "Where and when?"

"Do you know where Piney Branch Baptist Church is?"

"Well, of course. It's the biggest church in town."

"Park in the back parking lot and I'll meet you at the double doors. Service starts at 10:30."

"Ok, I'll be there. See you tomorrow."

"That'll be great, man. Tomorrow then," and Scott hung up.

Bill couldn't help but notice the excitement in Scott's voice. What had he gotten himself into?

Later that night, Bill called Victoria. His new phone sure was handy.

"Hello Jonas. Could I speak to Victoria?"

"Hey everybody, it's Bill!" Jonas shouted. It embarrassed Bill.

Bill could hear Jonas tell Edward, his youngest son, to get Victoria. The phone was being jostled around from the sound of things.

"Hello," and Bill melted. Her voice was soft and sweet. He had come to love the sound of it. He sat for a moment wishing he had never left her.

"Hello, are you there?"

"Yes, yes. I was realizing how much I miss you. I can't believe I left."

Victoria giggled. Bill told her about the flight home and what a great job Scott and Fred had done on the "cabin." They talked about small things, how much they missed each other.

"Scott invited me to church tomorrow." There was a silence on the other end. Bill thought he had lost the connection.

"Victoria? Are you still there?"

It was several seconds before she answered.

"Yes, yes. It's just I don't know what to say. It's great! Wonderful! I'm just surprised."

"Not as surprised as I am for saying yes. I can't remember the last time I was in a church, probably for a funeral or something. I'm a little nervous. I hope they won't kneel a lot. What should I wear?" Bill babbled on and on.

Victoria smiled and listened. She felt in her heart that God would not have let her fall in love with a man who wasn't a Christian. She knew God wouldn't let her down and could see his hand at work. As Bill continued to talk, Victoria whispered to Jonas to tell him about what was happening. Jonas grabbed Elizabeth's hand and began thanking God in prayer.

As Bill began winding down the conversation Victoria asked, "Bill, I know it's expensive to call here, but could you please call me tomorrow? I'd like to know what you thought of church and how it went. Please?"

"No problem. I'll talk to you tomorrow. Oh, one more thing. I just want you to know my feelings for you haven't changed."

"Stronger than ever," is all she said and hung up.

Bill laid the phone on the table and marveled at the technology. He slept like a dead man that night and was up before the alarm went off.

Bill arrived early to church. Good thing, because the parking lot was beginning to fill up. He spotted Scott through the glass doors. As Bill entered, a middle-aged man greeted him with a strong handshake and a "Good morning." Scott was standing next to a reception desk talking with a younger man, but quickly greeted Bill as soon as he spotted him.

"Hey Bill. Glad you made it."

"I'm here, kinda nervous and out of place, but I'm here."

"Don't worry. Nobody will bite you. Let me introduce you to some people." The two men approached the man Bill had been greeted by. "Bill, this is Pastor Carol Moore. Preacher, this is Bill August." The two men shook hands again. Carol leaned towards Bill and said, "I wouldn't let too many people know we have friends like him." They all laughed out loud, the preacher loudest of all. "Welcome Bill. I hope you enjoy my message as much," and he went back to greeting people.

"Let me find my wife, since I'll be busy during the service, you can sit with her," Scott told Bill. Scott went over to the young man he had been standing with and said something. "Come on Bill. She should be in the sanctuary." The place was huge. A large stage with chairs for the orchestra and choir was on their right as they entered from a side door.

There were eight sections of pews with aisles dividing each section. Hundreds of people were milling about, talking and looking for seats. Bill was overwhelmed. He had never been in a church of this size. The ceiling had to be forty feet above the floor and there was even a balcony. Scott spotted Sara sitting with her brother and his kids. Bill followed Scott to the pew.

"Mike, Sara, this is Bill." Sara looked surprised. Scott looked at Sara and said, "I told you he'd show up. I could tell by the sound of his voice." Sara blushed, not wanting Scott to go on. "Ah, Bill, I've got some things to take care of. I'll see you in a little while." Scott turned and moved out into the crowd.

Bill looked from Sara to Mike. "Take a seat, Bill," Mike said and the two shook hands.

"Why did you not expect me to show up?" Bill asked Sara.

"Scott has asked several people to come to church with him. Most don't show up. Fred has been a couple of times, but nothing steady. You know how Fred is. I guess most people can't believe Scott is even going to church." One of Mike's young boys climbed across the pew into Sara's lap. "Don't wallow me to death, boy."

"I can't believe how big this place is and bright. Most churches I've been in are dark and quiet," Bill told Sara.

"I guess for someone coming here for the first time it might seem big and overwhelming, but it's got a small church atmosphere about it. You'll see."

"When is Scott coming back?"

Sara explained that Scott was head of the security team.

"A security team? This is a church. Why do you need security?" Bill asked, still looking around.

"Well 9/11, for one thing, but the preacher has had threats against him. I know it sounds crazy, but some people. The Devil gets into them." Bill couldn't believe it. Sara continued, "You wouldn't believe the kind of wackos that show up here: con artists thinking a church is an easy mark, people who proclaim to be prophets, people who disagree with the Bible. All kinds," she explained.

"Why Scott?" Bill asked.

"I guess it takes one to know one," Mike butted in and they all laughed.

The side door opened up and Preacher Moore entered, followed by Scott at a short distance. The preacher eased around the large room shaking hands and talking to people. Bill didn't say anything to Sara or Mike, but Preacher Moore reminded him of Jimmy Swaggart. The orchestra began to play and the service started.

After the service, Sara invited Bill to lunch with them.

"There'll be a slew of us. One more won't hurt," she told him. "I just hope my nephews can behave."

Bill thought about Victoria's brothers. He was beginning to enjoy being around people again. A lot of things were sliding into place and it felt good.

***

The group sat at a large table with the adults at one end and the kids at the other. Bill and Scott managed to be seated across from each other. Once the waiter got the drink order, Bill handed Scott a folded up piece of paper. Scott knew what it was right away. Unfolding the check he realized Bill had made a mistake.

"This is way too much, man. It's twice what we agreed on. I know we went overboard on some things. Sara insisted on the rug, curtains and dishes, but not this much," Scott said, trying to hand the check back to Bill. Bill put up his hands in protest and leaned back in his chair, but Scott continued. "I've got a bill at the house. After lunch we'll get it and settle up."

"Will you shut up for a second?" Scott's hand recoiled as if Bill had hit him. "I couldn't believe or expect the job you all did. I could live there for a while and not build the house." Bill stopped, not knowing how far he wanted to go with this. "But I met someone on my trip, a local girl. And I may need a lot more room. I hope."

Scott smiled and Sara leaned in to listen.

"So keep it and enjoy."

Scott stuck the check in his pocket and told Bill they would talk about it later.

"So what did you think about the service?" Scott asked Bill.

"It was quite an experience. The choir was great and that trumpet solo…" Bill trailed off as he looked down the table to Scott and Sara's teenaged daughter, "was fantastic." Shay turned red and thanked him for the compliment. "Carol sure preached up a storm. Sometimes I thought he was speaking directly to me. I bought a CD to send to some friends in the Caymans."

The conversation rambled on from there. As lunch broke up, Bill asked Scott if they could talk some business. Scott told Bill he didn't do business on Sunday unless it couldn't wait. They agreed to meet at the Waffle House the next morning at 6:00.

On the way home, Scott and Sara talked about Bill.

"I expected someone more like Fred. Bill seems to have things a little more together," Sara told Scott.

"For a change, he isn't looking for a handout. Not that Fred is, but I can think of a few."

Sara and Scott had more than a few people come through their lives wanting something from them. Every time they tried to help someone, Scott and she ended up on the short end of the stick. Scott was bad to lend money or finance a car to someone and never be paid back. In fact, Sara had thought doing work for Bill was going to be a losing proposition, but it had worked out so far.

17

The two men met as planned. At breakfast, Bill explained to Scott that he wanted him to build his house.

"Look here, I know you don't know me very well, but from what I've seen, I want you to do my work. I'm willing to pay you well. From our conversation yesterday at lunch, I know you're slow right now. I guess 9/11 hurt everybody one way or the other."

Scott was worried that he might get sucked into another bad deal of some kind and if he did, he didn't want to try and explain what happened to Sara again. Scott studied the man across the table from him and asked, "How much? I mean we might as well get to the bottom line. And for how long?"

Bill knew how important these questions were. After all, they were talking about Scott's livelihood. If Scott worked for Bill, he would have to turn other work down if it came available.

"How about $2,000 a week? I'll pay cash for the first six months. It'll take me that long to set up a bona fide business. That will include all of your equipment. I'll pay for fuel; you cover the rest."

"What do you mean by 'business'?" Scott asked?

"I want to set up a corporation for tax reasons and I've got an idea for a future business."

$2,000 a week for 40 hours. Scott did the math. That was $50 an hour. Not bad, not great. When times were booming he got twice that, but times weren't booming. Since September, business was way off and NAFTA hadn't helped, either. Ross Perot had been right. Most of the plant work had come to a halt as they moved to Mexico or shut down.

"When do I have to let you know?"

"Right now."

"Right now? I wanted to talk it over with Sara. You think it'll last six months?"

"Look, what I'm about to say stays at this table. You make up your mind right now and you can start drawing a paycheck."

Bill knew Scott didn't have any work for the week. He also heard at lunch how strapped for cash he was. Several jobs hadn't paid yet and Scott didn't know when they would. This was part of the joys of being self-employed. The end of the month was coming up fast and so were his bills.

Scott pondered awhile. "What about help? You and I can't do everything." He was trying to buy some time.

"Any help we need, I'll pay them, no problem."

"Bill, you got me against the ropes. How do I know you can afford to pay me? Do you really have that kind of money?" Scott knew the questions were hard, but he had to know. Bill extended his hand across the table and said, "I give you my word."

Scott looked hard at Bill for several seconds, reached for his hand and said, "Good enough," and shook hands.

Now down to business.

Bill and Scott spent the rest of the day together. They drove to Maggie Valley to look at several log houses. As they entered the first model, a large man approached them.

"Can I help you boys?"

"I'm thinking about building a log home," Bill said, handing the fellow a floor plan of what he wanted.

The salesman proceeded to tell Bill how great his logs were and blah, blah, blah. He sounded just like the salesman at Home Depot. The guy hardly drew a breath. After going on and on, he finally told Bill the price.

"This is a bunch of crap. Let's get out of here," Scott said, loud enough to be heard throughout the room.

"Come on, Bill. I can't take any more of this blowhard." Both Bill's and the salesman's jaws dropped and Scott was out the door headed for the truck.

"What'd I say? What'd I say?" the salesman asked Bill.

Bill shrugged and left.

"Damn, Scott, I thought he was giving me a deal," Bill said as they drove out the parking lot.

"That guy was some kind of carpetbagger. I'll bet you wouldn't have got what you paid for anyway. Let's go see a local guy I know."

Scott took Bill to a sawmill just outside of Brevard. The place was a mess, sawdust and shavings everywhere. The small homemade banner with the name of the mill flapped in the breeze and the sound of the motor and blade were deafening. Scott went into a small, dark office. He came out minutes later to find Bill mesmerized, watching the logs being sawn into rough-cut planks.

"Hey! Bill, come here," Scott yelled over the noise.

Bill stepped into the office.

"This is Biggen. This is Bill." Scott had to yell above the sound of the saw.

"Yeah, Scott here said you needed some logs."

All Bill could do was nod his head. Biggin's greasy hair was plastered to his forehead with a ball cap sitting all the way back on his head. The guy was so big and fat only one strap from his overalls could be snapped.

As he arose from behind the desk, both Bill and Scott had to back out the door to keep from being crushed.

They followed Biggen around the wood yard like a couple of puppies. About a hundred yards from the office, he pointed to a neatly stacked pile of square logs.

"Is that what you're looking for?" Biggen asked as he spit out a wad of tobacco.

Bill looked down at the pile of nasty, wet mess. *How could he have all that in his mouth and still talk?* he wondered.

"Well, maybe. How big a house will they make?" Scott asked?

"Let me think,"Biggen looked up and counted on his fingers, then went into a long explanation. "This ole Florida fellow came in here and wanted them cut for a house he was gonna build. He even gave me a deposit. Ain't never been back. I think he said something about 2,000 - 2,500 feet. Will that do?"

Bill and Scott looked at each other and nodded.

"How much," Bill asked.

Just then the saw at the mill bogged down. "If'n them dumb SOB's stall that motor again I'll kick their tail ends!" Biggen yelled, looking back at the mill. "You can't get good help nowadays. White boys won't work and the Mexicans can't speak English." Bill wasn't sure if Biggen was speaking English.

"Ten thousand for the whole load."

"Five and you load 'em on our trailer," Scott blurted out.

"No way, not a penny less than seventy-five hundred," Biggen said, loading another wad of tobacco in his mouth.

"Let's go, Bill," Scott said, jumping off the pile of logs.

"Now wait a minute, boys. How's about sixty-five hundred, cash and that's as best I can do."

"If you'll load 'em for us, we got a deal."

Biggen spat big and wiped his lips with the back of his hand. "Deal." They all shook and told the massive being they would be back in a week to pick them up.

"You were right, Scott. That guy in Maggie was an idiot. But this guy was the nastiest human being I ever saw."

"You ought to see his wife," Scott said and they both started laughing.

The two made a few more stops before Scott dropped Bill back at the Waffle House to pick up his truck.

"Hey, are you sure you don't want to come to my house for dinner? Sara's a great cook and it's free entertainment with the kids and all," Scott asked Bill again.

"No, you wore me out. I think I'll go home and crash. I'll see you in the morning," Bill declined, thinking more about calling Victoria. He couldn't wait to get home to call her. It was dark when Bill got back to his cabin. The days were getting shorter and cooler as it got closer to winter. After a shower and light dinner, he got his little book out.

Bill kept a very accurate account of all his money, how much was deposited at which banks and more importantly, how much he had spent and on what. There were small notations like "watch" or "breakfast," even "gas" for his truck. By the time Bill finished his paperwork, it was time to call Victoria.

He told her all about going to church, again. It made her so happy that he was making an effort to understand what she believed in. When the conversation reached a lull, Victoria said, "Daddy wants to talk to you," and Jonas' voice came through the speaker.

"Bill, hold on a second while I go outside."

Bill could hear Jonas walking through the house with the TV on in the background and the kids talking. He hoped it wasn't something to do with Pop Pop.

"Bill, you there?"

"Yeah, is there a problem?"

"No and yes."

"Is Victoria ok? Nothing's wrong, is there? Is Pop Pop back, or..."

Jonas cut him off. "Bill, just listen. Did you put money in my bank account?"

"Yes."

"Why?"

"Let me think, why." It was a question Bill wasn't expecting but should have. "I saw how hard you worked and you became my friend, no questions asked. You didn't ask me for anything or take anything for granted. I had one of the best times of my life with you and your family. You shared what you had with me, so I shared something with you."

Bill's explanation caught Jonas by surprise. Jonas was sure it had to do with Victoria, but he could tell by Bill's voice he was sincere. Bill continued, "Some of us are blessed in different ways. You have your family. I don't have any and I have very few friends. The ones I have I like doing things for them to make life a little easier. I've come into some money recently, so I share the wealth."

Jonas didn't know what to say. All he could come up with was, "Thank you, Bill. Believe me when I say no one has ever done anything like that for me."

"You're welcome. Enjoy," and Bill hung up the phone and began to cry. This was the first time in his life he was able to help someone, even if it wasn't his money.

18

Bill called Scott the next morning and told him he was bringing over a motorcycle for him to work on.

On the way to the warehouse to pick up his bike Bill thought about how good things were going. He had made some friends—friends who would be friends through thick and thin, not fair weather friends. Life was looking up. That was, until he turned onto the road where the storage complex was and his heart sank.

Parked all around the entrance were sheriff patrol cars. But the black, large, four-door Fords looked more menacing. It wasn't like Bill hadn't foreseen this day; he just didn't figure driving into it. He went back over everything in his mind to recall how well he covered his tracks.

Bill pulled up to the gate like everything was normal. A deputy greeted him with a, "Can I help you?"

"Yeah, I rent a warehouse here. Is there a problem?" Bill asked.

The deputy turned his head and talked into the microphone on his chest. A young man in a dark suit walked up to Bill's window. "I'm Agent Bishop with the FBI. Can I see some ID please?"

"Can I?" asked Bill. "Only kidding," and he handed Bishop his driver's license.

While studying the photo ID, Bishop asked, "What storage unit are you currently renting?"

"313, What's going on?" Bill asked the agent, as if he didn't know.

"Mr. August, I'll need to speak with you in the manager's office. Please park your truck outside the fence and come in."

The deputy motioned Bill where to park and escorted him to the office. Bill started to get butterflies in his stomach. There were a ton of cops around. He felt as if he were surrounded. These guys were professionals. *Surely I can't outsmart them. Just be cool and hope you didn't leave anything behind.* That night flashed across Bill's mind. He was trying to think if he had forgotten one small thing. Then he was opening the door to the office.

The agent was seated behind the manager's desk and asked Bill to have a seat. There was only one chair in the room and it was right in front of the desk. The deputy stood next to the door and behind the chair. Bill tried to relax. *Remember, they don't know what happened,* he thought.

"How long have you rented number 313?"

"Oh, I don't know, maybe 18 months or better," Bill answered. "What's this all about?"

"What do you keep in the unit?"

"I'm not answering any more questions 'til you tell me what's going on here." Bill crossed his arms and stared at the agent.

Bishop shuffled some papers and without looking up said, "Several men employed by Wells Fargo stole an armored truck. They emptied the contents and parked it in a unit several spaces from yours. We are presently investigating the crime. That is about all I can share with you, Mr. August."

"Oh," was all Bill said. "Well. I've got some motor-cycles, tools, clothes, a few household goods."

"Thank you. Would you mind if we take a look?"

"Not at all. Come on, I'll show you."

The agent stood and the two men exited the office. As Bill led the way, Agent Bishop motioned two men to follow. One carried a toolbox, the other a large flashlight.

Bill unlocked the door and raised it. "There you go," and waved the men into the warehouse.

The FBI agents turned on flashlights and entered the dark unit. Bill reached for the light switch and turned on the light. "Is that better?" They surely were a talkative bunch.

***

The light lit up the space. No one paid attention to the motorcycles sitting in the middle of the floor. One of the agents began pulling on the drawers of the locked toolbox. Bill threw him the key. They searched everywhere and everything.

"I have a few questions, Mr. August," said Bishop in a monotone voice.

"Ask away there, Agent Bishop."

"Why the refrigerator?"

"I work on my bikes in here, so I keep food and water in there."

"Do you sleep here?"

"I have, but not lately."

"Why?"

"Like I said, I work on my bikes here. Sometimes I lose track of time and I'll crash here instead of going home."

Bishop thought about what Bill had just said. That explained the mattress leaned against the back door. But why all the empty boxes?

"Have you ever seen these men here?" Agent Bishop handed Bill some black and white photos. Bill studied the pictures for some time, not because of Bishop's question, but in case he should ever see one. But how would they ever know about me if the FBI doesn't? Be very careful.

"No," and then added, "I've never seen them around here," which was the truth, except for that rainy night.

"Are you sure? You looked like you might have recognized them."

"Absolutely. To be honest, I've never seen anybody here, rarely even the manager."

"There are two round holes cut in the front and rear doors. What are they for?"

"I don't know. They were here when I rented this place. There was some kind of plug in them," Bill explained as he pulled the door down a little to reveal the holes. The plug wasn't in the door.

"Well, it's gone now. Maybe the one in the back door is still there."

Bill and the agent walked to the back door. Bill moved the mattress and pointed to the plug. Agent Bishop pulled a small plastic bag from his pocket and handed it to Bill.

"Is this the one for the other door?"

Bill looked it over, knowing it was.

"It looks like it. I guess it could be. It's not something I checked on or anything."

"Has it ever come out before?"

"I don't think so. Not with me, anyway," Bill told the agent. First mistake, Bill thought.

"Where were you the night of October 16th?"

"Shoot, man, I can't remember that far back. That's been, what, two or three weeks ago. I've slept since then."

"Try to remember. It's very important," Agent Bishop urged Bill.

It surely was important. It was the night Bill became a multimillionaire and it was very important to Agent Bishop's career.

"Hell, I can't remember."

One of the other agents handed Bishop a small slip of paper. He glanced at it and said to Bill, "We found a receipt from a grocery store dated October 14th for a salad and sandwich. Does that ring a bell?"

"Not really. I stopped for food a lot before coming here. It might have been from the last time I ate here. I just don't know."

"You haven't been here recently," Bishop said. Bill knew this was more of a statement than question.

"I finished that bike and the other one runs fine. No need." Bill pointed to the old Norton. "The BMW hardly ever needs any work. The Norton needs to be worked on almost every time I ride it."

With the way Bill was looking at the motorcycles, the agent knew Bill wasn't lying.

Bill noticed one of the agents measuring something in the toolbox. It was the hole saw Bill had used to drill the door with. No wait, he had taken several hole saws to work and he was sure he had taken that one. How sure? He couldn't remember, but pretty sure. Bill tried not to notice what the agent was doing, but it was hard.

The three agents stepped outside and talked to each other in low voices. Bill couldn't hear what they were saying. One agent shook his head from side to side. Bill took this for a good sign.

***

Bill looked around at what had been his world and wondered if he had overlooked something else. The gloves and mirror were buried with the money. His mind raced over that night trying to remember if anything was missed.

"Well, did you find anything?" Bishop asked his two comrades.

"Nothing, sir. Everything he said about eating, working and sleeping here was the truth, as far as the evidence goes. He was also truthful about not being here in a while. Did you find anything, Smith?"

"No. I thought that drill had made the holes in the door, but it was the wrong size. The plug could have come out when the door was raised or lowered. We already checked for fingerprints but came up empty. I think we can cross this one off the list. Besides, his background and profile don't fit. What do you think, Sir?"

"I don't think he was involved, but still…" and Bishop went over in his mind several things. The boxes, the holes in the door and how Bill studied the mug shots, although the three men in jail never mentioned a fourth in all the interviews.

"You suspect everybody, Sir."

"That's my job," and Bishop looked at Bill standing in the building. "Mr. August, could you step out here, please?"

Bill did as he was asked.

"We want to thank you for answering our questions and your cooperation. If you think of anything, please call me." Bishop handed Bill a business card. "I may have more questions for you. How can I reach you?" Bill gave him his cell number.

"Hey, can I ask you a few questions, Agent Bishop?"

"Why?"

Bill stumbled for a moment, then said, "I guess I just wanted to know what's going on and where I stand."

"Well, Mr. August, if you didn't have any involvement you should know where you stand."

Bill felt as if he had backed himself into a corner. Maybe he wasn't as cool and smart as he thought. Bishop continued to probe Bill's face and body movements. Bill was becoming more and more uncomfortable.

"In that case, I'd like to say it's been nice talking to you, but under the circumstances…"

Bishop dropped his scan of Bill. As far as Bishop was concerned, nothing pointed to Bill being involved. This man's unit was free of any physical evidence, but (there was that but) what about all of those boxes and the hole in the doors? What did he use those boxes for? And the manager couldn't remember if the holes were in the doors before he rented it to Mr. August.

Bishop put a star next to Bill's name on his list. He was going to have to look into Bill August a little deeper.

"Officer, escort Mr. August back to his truck. Thank you again, Mr. August."

Bill responded, "I came here to get my motorcycle. I'd like to go riding today and I need to lock my building." It was more of a statement than a question and it caught Bishop off guard. Bishop thought for a moment. Maybe he was wrong about Bill August. "Okay, Officer, allow him to do so." Bishop turned and walked away.

Bill looked at his truck parked outside the gate in the same spot as always. He wondered if he had locked it or not and if not would Bishop go through it. This worried him, under the driver's seat were the notebooks containing all the money information. Plus, had he left any evidence in the truck. Somehow he had to stop at the truck on the way out without calling attention to his actions. All this and more went through his mind as the young deputy officer escorted him to his unit.

Bishop watched from the office door as Bill prepared to ride. Bill locked his unit and the officer inserted an orange zip tie through the lock.

"What's that for?" Bill asked.

"Lets us know we already searched this unit."

Bill looked down the row of units and realized that most had already been searched.

"And I thought you were picking on me." Bill smiled at the officer and started his motorcycle. Slowly he rode down the narrow alley way and out the gate. He stopped at his truck and dismounted the machine. Opening the door of the truck, it wasn't locked, he reached in as if to retrieve something. After making sure the truck was locked, he got back on his bike. As he rode off Bill waved to Bishop still standing in the window. He did not wave back.

The police officer walked up to Bishop. "What do you think?"

"I don't know. He's different, for sure. There isn't any physical connection we can find. Damn, I didn't get his place of employment." Bishop went into the manager's office and the police officer cross number 313 off his list.

Bishop was stumped. None of the three suspects were talking. All of them claimed the money was in the truck when they left, but it was empty now. Somebody was lying, but whom? Bishop knew he was going to have to offer a deal to one of them to get him to roll on the others. But which one? Bishop had had the whole storage complex under surveillance since the manager reported finding the uniforms. Bill was right about hardly anybody being seen around here. Bishop guessed that's why the robbers had picked this place. In fact, two tenants had passed away and the manager didn't even know it. He had just thought they were late on their rent.

As Bill motored down the road, he hoped to never hear from Agent Bishop again.!

'Let's go back to county, I want to interview our boys again," Bishop said to the deputy.

***

The interview room was brightly lit but small. David Rakes sat at the only table, facing the one way window. None of the three men had requested an attorney yet, even though they were given the opportunity to do so.

Agent Bishop observed Mr. Rakes through the glass. The man sitting in the room looked very tired and in need of a shave and bath. The orange coveralls were too big and the sleeves and pant legs were rolled up, about six inches.

Bishop was confused, none of this robbery made sense, well some of it did. He could understand why they did it, seventeen million was a lot of money for anybody. But why did they leave Rake's partner alive?

And the big question, where had the money gone? The truck was a clean sweep, nothing left in there. Whoever took the money left nothing—not even a hair. The CSI guys said it must have been vacuumed out. Where had he seen a vacuum, which warehouse? The only reason they had found the truck was the warehouse owner came across the uniform in the dumpster. Not much was adding up and why hadn't these three left the area right away.

All three were arrested together at the warehouse and they all claimed the money was in the truck. Bishop did believe them on this point. Something wasn't right and Bishop was going to get to the bottom of it. He had a list of a lot of small things he needed to figure out first. Things like the truck key being found in David Rakes' uniform pants pocket when all the suspects claimed they were in the truck.

Sid and Mark couldn't remember David putting the uniform in the dumpster. And the lock was full of super glue, but when the suspects came back to the warehouse and the lock opened, no one was surprised. Bishop had put the same number master lock on the unit so their key would fit. Up to this point none of the suspects had mentioned anything about the lock. Either someone was double crossing or there was a fourth person involved.

Bishop entered the room and sat down facing David Rakes. He laid a pad and pencil between them on the table.

"Thanks for agreeing to this interview, Mr. Rakes."

"Well it's not like I had much else going on."

Agent Bishop looked at the man and knew Rakes was at the end of his rope.

"I know I've asked some of these questions before, but just bear with me, I'm just trying to clear up a few things."

Rakes nodded his head too tired to speak.

"Could you give me a little more detail on why you did it, Mr. Rakes."

David dropped his head further, almost to the table. He couldn't look at Bishop.

"Yea sure. I make, made eighteen dollars an hour after seventeen long years. I get six paid holidays and two weeks' vacation. My wife left me for some younger rich guy, hell I can't even afford a new car. I figured seventeen mill, one for each shitty year."

Most of what David said was true. His wife didn't leave him for a rich guy. She left because he started hanging out with two low life's, Sid and Mark. And they were dragging him down, drinking and what not.

Bishop had already spoken to David's wife. Everything had checked out true.

"Ok Mr. Rakes, ok." Bishop didn't want to get him upset and changed the subject. "Mr. Sidney and Mr.

Austin don't remember you putting the uniform in the dumpster."

"I must have. I was so giddy at that point, I just don't remember."

Fact was both of the other men said Rakes had thrown it on the seat of the truck.

"Do you recollect who locked the warehouse door," Bishop asked?

"It was Sid because Mark had grabbed the car keys from him and said something about not wanting Sid to fall asleep while driving."

And now came the big question, "What do you think happened to all that money….."

David Rakes let his head go all the way to the table, he drew in a breath and let out a sob, "Man I just don't know."

"Think, that amount of cash doesn't disappear into thin air." Bishop paused for a moment, "if you could help me out a little it would go a long way in court."

And think he did. If he gave this guy something, anything, maybe the judge would go easy on him. Of course, what would he do after he got out of jail? But that didn't enter his mind. What could he say that might help his case some? He had to point his finger at someone, but who? And then Bishop's question about who locked the door came into his small brain. That was a strange thing to ask. Why, did Sid leave it unlocked? The light went on. Sid, of course. He always acted a little slow, but it was just that an act. And he had that Mexican brother-in-law. It had to be them, who else, Mark maybe? Sure, they were in it together, both against me. That had to be it.

Rakes looked up, "How can you help me?"

This was what Bishop was hoping for.

"You give me something I can use and I'll talk to the judge. The important thing is we need to recover the money. But remember it's got to be good useful information, because to be honest, Mr. Rakes, a lot of this falls on you."

Rakes looked around the room. He knew his new digs would be a lot smaller.

"You need to check up on Sid's brother-in-law."

"Is that it," Bishop was disappointed. Did Rakes think he was stupid? They already had and neither could be reached. But they were still checking into them. No stone left unturned.

"I can't think of anything else, I just can't," and David Rakes began to cry.

Bishop stood, touched Rakes shoulder, grabbed the pencil and pad and went out.

***

"Not very useful, huh Agent Bishop," said the young deputy, who had been assigned to escort Bishop.

"Well yes and no, Deputy Esquivel. I guess we better dig up the sister and brother-in- law."

"Yea, blame it on the Mexican," said the deputy and Bishop smiled at the young man. "Well prepare yourself, the reporters are out front." And the two men headed for the front door.

Hendersonville wasn't like a big city where twenty or thirty reporters would be waiting and yelling. There were only six and when Bishop held up his hand they became quite.

"We have three suspects in custody and are in the process of apprehending two more. This is an open and shut, almost a textbook type robbery." And again the vacuum cleaner came to mind. "I'll take three questions."

Why did August stop at his truck.

"Have you found the money," one reporter yelled out.

Did I see a vacuum in August's unit, no.

"No, but we will."

I do suspect everybody.

"Have you charged Robert Passmore, the guard found in the forest."

Of course everybody bothers me.

"No he is not a suspect and yes he will recover from his ordeal."

Where did I see that vacuum.

"Who and where are the other two suspects?"

Maybe I shouldn't suspect everyone.

"Are you kidding and that was three," and Bishop and Esquivel walked to their car.

I've got alot of work to do.

19

Bill and Scott rode motorcycles the rest of that day, stopping here and there, checking on different things for the house. Bill never mentioned talking to Agent Bishop, but he did start checking the newspaper for any articles pertaining to the heist. For a few days, it had been the talk of the town. Now everyone had moved on to the next big event. But not Bill, he needed to stay as up-to-date on any new information that was released.

The closing on the lot wouldn't be until the next Friday giving the new friends plenty of time to get everything in order. After getting the permits and setting up delivery dates, they headed for the Parkway.

"Scott, have you ever been to the Cayman Islands?" Bill asked as the two men sat at an overlook.

"Sure have. A friend of mine and I went diving a couple of time. I took Sara and her kids not long after we were married. It's real nice, but expensive."

"You want to go with me in about a week?"

"I'd love to, but there's no way we can afford it right now."

"Ah, come on. I already got a condo rented. All you'll have to get is the tickets for a flight. We can eat in, so food won't cost much. It'll be a great vacation on the cheap."

"I don't know. Me and Sara will have to talk it over."

Scott and Sara decided to go. They hadn't had a vacation in some time. Bill flew down several days before them. Victoria was waiting at the airport for him. They embraced, Bill taking in her scent and beauty. They had missed each other and held the embrace for some time. Bill rented a car because Victoria had come by taxi. Jonas needed the truck for work.

"Well, where are your friends, Bill?" He could listen to her speak all day. Between the English and Caribbean accents in her voice she had a dialect all her own.

"They couldn't get a flight out until tomorrow. Let's go to your house."

"Ok. Daddy should be home for lunch shortly."

"I can't wait to see him."

"He can't wait to see you. That's all he's been talking about," Victoria told him as they got in the rental. As soon as the door shut, Victoria leaned over and waited for a kiss.

"I've missed you too much," Bill told her. He knew it was a short amount of time, but he was going to ask Jonas for his blessing to marry Victoria, if she would have him.

"I don't want to think about you leaving again, but it's always on my mind," and her eyes welled up with tears.

"Let's enjoy the next week, make the most of the time we have."

Victoria smiled and kissed him.

***

Jonas was already home when Bill and Victoria pulled in the driveway. Jonas met Bill at the door of the car, grabbed his hand and pulled Bill to him. He hugged Bill and whispered in his ear, "Thanks again."

Bill asked Jonas to set up another fishing trip, this time for three: Bill, Scott and his son.

"Bad news, Bill. This may be one of the Captain's last trips. He plans on retiring in a week or so," Jonas explained.

"Why, I'll have to talk to him. He's way too young to retire." They both laughed, knowing the Captain was close to 80.

"I guess he's fished enough. Time to let someone else catch a few of the big ones," Jonas told Bill.

"What's he going to do with the boat and tackle?" Bill asked.

"He told me he was going to sell everything, use the money to live on and take it easy."

Bill's mind began to roll over an idea about all this. "We'll see. I've got company coming. I need to stock the condo and make sure I have everything. Victoria, you reckon you could give me a hand?"

Jonas frowned and Bill asked if there was a problem.

"I would rather the two of you not be at your place alone."

Bill thought for a second. "What if we take one of the boys with us? Would that be okay?"

"That would be good. Thanks, Bill. But take both."

Victoria looked at Bill. She was proud of him for respecting her father.

On the way to the condo, Bill quizzed Victoria about her dad.

"How good is your dad at fishing?"

"Even when he was drinking, he was one of the best mates around. All the different boat owners wanted him to mate for them when he was sober."

"What about now?"

"He won't go out on a boat where the guys are fishing and drinking. He tells me if you're going fishing, fish. If you're going drinking, drink. He doesn't like when people combine the two. Besides, the Bible said not to hang around drunkards and he doesn't need the temptation."

"Good point. Have you ever drank?"

Victoria hung her head. "When I dated Pop Pop I did everything—drank, drugs, wild parties." She hung her head lower. "I'm not a virgin, you know. The night of the shooting, Pop Pop wanted me to have sex with him and two other girls. I almost did it, too. I don't know what stopped me, because I was pretty messed up. Maybe I shouldn't tell you all this."

"No, it's okay. We all have a past."

"You're right, we all have a past and I know beyond a doubt that I'm forgiven. Sometimes it's hard to walk the path, especially since I've tasted the fruit. What I'm trying to say is, I love you and want you. But I'm going to wait."

"Don't worry, girl, just chill. No pressure here."

"Thanks. Church tonight?"

Bill would go anywhere with her, but there was more to it. Ever since that Sunday morning with Scott, Bill hadn't missed a chance to attend. There were subtle changes in him. He felt more uplifted and treated people better. Most of the time Bill avoided crowds, but he felt comfortable with the crowd at church.

"I wouldn't miss going. Can I pick you up?"

Victoria giggled. "Sure."

Victoria's brothers, Jay and Joey, sat in the back seat of the car listening to every word that was said. Some they understood, others not. First graders only have a limited understanding of adult talk, but one was surely going to tell Daddy about the kiss and ask what happens at wild parties, but Jonas already knew everything. It didn't take the boys long to warm up to Bill after they stopped for ice cream.

Bill didn't notice the stares from other people at TCBY. A white man with a light skinned, young, black girl and two small children. Victoria did notice and she deliberately grabbed and held onto Bill's hand. Bill put his arm around her on the way to the car. Life was great.

The next morning, Bill went to see the Captain.

"Ahoy matey!" Bill hollered to the old man working in the bottom of the boat. "Remember me?"

"Yes, you're the nut who lets the big marlins go."

"That's me. Can we talk awhile?"

The Captain looked at Bill. "Sure, time for a break. What's on your mind?"

Bill smiled and plopped down in the fighting chair. "Jonas said you're going to retire and sell the boat."

"Ain't no secrets no more. Yeah, I'm getting too old for this, but I still love it. That old woman of mine is hounding me about retiring. Probably put me in an early grave." Looking out to sea. the Captain continued, "I always figured I'd die out there, not drool myself to death in a clean bed."

"Captain, I've got something I'd like you to think about. What if you didn't sell off all the boat?" Bill could see the confusion on the old salt's face. "Now, hear me out. What if I buy, say, two-thirds of the boat? You keep a third and we let Jonas run it. That way you get a little money up front and some from every trip. You'll still have an income and you get to go out when you feel like it. It all hinges on if you think Jonas is up to the challenge."

"What do you think?" The Captain asked Bill.

"I wouldn't have mentioned it if I had any doubt."

"I'm going fishing tonight. I'll think it over. I do my best thinking while I'm fishing, you know."

***

That night after dinner, Jonas and Bill walked down to the docks behind Jonas' house. Jonas pointed out different sport fishers tied up at the pier. He knew which had gas or diesel engines, how fast they went and how they handled in heavy seas.

"You know a lot about them, don't you, Jonas?"

"I've been around them my whole life. My dad taught me to fish. You know, I lost my boat when I was a drinkin man."

"I didn't know you had a boat."

"It wasn't big or anything, but it made me a living. I sure miss it." Jonas looked upward. "Maybe someday, if God sees fit, I'll have another."

They walked down the dock in silence, the water lapping against the boats' hulls.

"Jonas, I've got to ask you something important. I'm not one to beat around the bush, so I'll come right to the point. I would like to marry Victoria, if she'll have me, but I wanted to ask you first."

Jonas stopped in his tracks. He was floored. He knew they liked each other and got along great, but Bill hadn't publicly professed his love of Christ yet. Jonas didn't know this man well enough, so he did the only thing he knew to do. He began to pray.

"Oh Lord, please help me. I've made so many mistakes. Guide me from another one. Is this the man for my baby girl? Will he be good to her and treat her well? Will she love and honor him the rest of her life? Please, oh Lord, hear this prayer from your humble servant. Amen."

Bill waited for some response from Jonas. He had hung his head and Bill took this for a bad omen.

The moon was beginning to rise over the bay. As Jonas looked up from his prayer, bait fish jumped out of the water. Then, right in front of the moon a huge marlin breached the surface. Jonas' eyes grew to the size of silver dollars. A grin spread across his face. Bill hadn't a clue as to what was going on in Jonas' mind. The marlin took both men by surprise.

"Yes. Yes, Bill, if she'll have you."

"Thank you," and Bill let out a howl at the moon.

"Is everything all right, boys?" Elizabeth asked from down the dock. All she could see were Bill and Jonas hugging each other and dancing in a circle.

"Yes, Mom, never better. We'll be right there," Jonas called to her.

Later that night, after returning to his condo, Bill went out on the beach. The ocean was only yards from his back door. He pulled a chair up close to the small breakers and sat down. The air was still warm, but he could feel the coolness of the water on his skin. The full moon was bright and reflected off the water. It had always amazed him that the waves never ceased to wash up on shore.

Bill's mind wandered. It had been an unbelievable five weeks. So many things had happened—most of which had changed his life. He looked up at the stars and couldn't help but think about God. He had always believed in God because he knew man did not or could not control things, but he had never thought about God like Victoria or Jonas or Scott did. Every time he went to church and Pastor Carol preached, it was like he was talking directly to Bill, but his two biggest questions still hadn't been answered. "Why Amber?" and "What about the money?"

Bill felt guilty about both. Amber because of Victoria. Falling in love with Victoria made him question his love for Amber. Had he ever loved her the way he loves Victoria? He and Amber never talked about God. Amber was into the New Age thing and Bill never gave it much thought. He just knew that if it made Amber happy and didn't hurt anybody, it was okay with him. Victoria, on the other hand, believed in God with all her heart. Not a day or hour went by that she didn't thank Him for something—giving Him all the credit. Victoria's life had been way harder than Amber's, yet she was more thankful than Amber ever was. Victoria's conviction and faith helped her through everything and gave her peace. It was something Bill admired greatly.

Then there was the money. He was pulled in two directions about it. His first instinct was to keep it. It was basically thrown at him. He had never dreamed of having this much money. As of yet, it hadn't caused him any problems. In fact, he was able to solve a few with it. He had helped Jonas out and now Scott. How many others could he help if he tried? Yet, there was a lingering problem. What if Agent Bishop figured out what happened? He knew Bishop wasn't a dummy. If Bill got caught, then he would let a lot of people down. They would think he was just a charade. That would break Victoria's heart. He couldn't let that happen.

Bill looked up at the stars and began to pray for the first time in his life.

20

Scott and Sara arrived. They loved the condo and were surprised at how nice it was. Bill and Victoria had stocked the kitchen with food and snacks. Sara was cautious at first. She always looked on the down side of things. Of course, people always taking advantage of her and Scott didn't help.

The kids didn't even unpack. They rushed into their swimsuits and headed for the beach. As soon as they stepped onto the sand, they began to run. Shay and Jeff spent the rest of the day in the warm, clear water.

Scott couldn't help it, but he kept thanking Bill, which embarrassed both of them. Sara set up command in the small kitchen.

"Bill, there's no way you did this all yourself. I think a woman's hand is in here somewhere, somehow," she quizzed Bill.

Bill smiled and began to blush. He had only eluded to Victoria, but hadn't told anyone about her. There was a knock on the door. Scott was closest and answered it. When Scott opened the door, there stood a tall black man, two small boys and a beautiful young woman.

"Hello. You must be Scott. I'm Jonas," and the two boys rushed by Scott. It surprised Scott so much that all he did was watch them go by.

"Sara, Scott, this is Victoria and her dad, Jonas." Victoria put her arm around Bill's waist and kissed him on the cheek. "And wrapped around my legs are Thing One and Thing Two." Bill looked down and asked the boy on his left leg, "You are Thing One, right?"

"No, I'm Thing Two." Then the other one said, "No, I'm Thing Two," and the fight was on. Jonas looked at Bill and shook his head. "Do you always have to get them started? Someday I'm going to drop them off here after feeding them chocolate for lunch. We'll see how you like it."

"That'll be all right. I've got plenty of duct tape."

Sara deduced Bill and Victoria's relationship right away. "This is a surprise. Bill never said anything about you to us. We should have known when he came home from here a couple of weeks ago. Scott said he changed. We thought it was from going to church with us."

"You think he's changed? You should be around my Victoria. She smiles and laughs again," Jonas told Sara and everybody started talking at once.

Scott and Sara's daughter, Shay, took up with Thing One and Two. The adults sat on the patio and watch the kids play in the surf. They talked for hours and munched on different things as Sara whipped them up. Jonas left for a short time to get Elizabeth. Bill suggested they all go out for dinner. Rounding up a crowd this size to get ready was an ordeal in itself. It would take some time.

Bill called ahead so a table would be ready and they all packed into two cars.

Everybody was having a great time eating and telling stories. The men made plans to go fishing the next day. Bill noticed Jonas now had a cell phone that he called the Captain on. Bill also noticed Jonas was somewhat embarrassed to use it. Jonas looked at Bill and slightly held the phone in his direction and nodded. Bill just smiled.

The women, of course, made plans to go shopping. Elizabeth and Victoria promised to show Sara all the local haunts.

"Oh honey, the tourist stores take all your money. We'll show you the best places," Elizabeth told Sara.

It was after 10:00 before they got out of the restaurant. They all piled into the car and truck for the ride home. Fishing started early the next morning, so they called it a night. Thing One and Two made fun of their sister kissing Bill good night. Bill and Victoria held hands until the truck pulled away.

Shay and Jeff were watching TV while Bill and Scott stood on the balcony.

"Man, Bill, she sure is a looker," Scott said of Victoria.

"Yes, but there's more than that. I'm going to ask her to marry me."

"Are you sure? Have you asked Jonas? He seems pretty protective."

"I asked him. It went well."

"It had to go better than when I asked Sara's parents. I'll tell you about it someday."

Bill let it drop. Fred had already told him about Scott and Sara, at least the parts he knew.

"I'm going to bed. Five A.M. comes early," Bill yawned and went inside.

Scott sat on the balcony to think things out. He knew Bill was hiding something, but what? It had been a long day. Sitting in the dark with a warm breeze felt good, especially since he knew it was going to be a long winter.

As Scott was getting in bed Sara asked, "How much was dinner?"

"I don't know."

"What do you mean?"

"Bill took care of it before we all sat down. I don't know how, but he did. Tip and everything."

"That's not right. Scott, you need to give him some money. It must have been three or four hundred dollars and with the exchange rate it had to be close to $1,000 US."

"Take a breath, Baby. Don't worry about it. I'll talk to him tomorrow."

"Remember, we're on a budget."

"You remember, you're the one going shopping."

"How much do you think the fishing trip will cost?"

"It's usually around $500 and another $50 to tip the mate. The $500 will be split four ways."

"Four ways?"

"Yeah, Bill, Jonas, me and Bill said to bring Jeff. So that'll be about $300 for us."

"I guess that will be okay if we don't eat out again."

"Sara, try to enjoy yourself. It'll all work out. It always does," Scott told her and he thought, "The world will turn."

Sara couldn't understand. Scott never worried about things that were important, but she had many sleepless nights over the business. When it was booming before 9/11 she worried about getting all the work done, paying bills, taxes, payroll and the office work. Now that things slowed down she just worried about money.

Scott, on the other hand, never seemed to worry about anything. He'd get up every morning and go to work. Whether it was a job, working on equipment, or bidding jobs, there was always something to do. Scott was older than Sara and had grown up in a different era. Maybe that was the reason Scott was like he was. As sleep set in Sara's mind began to wander. Bill seemed like a nice enough guy. He was attending church, but where was he getting his money? Scott said Bill had told him from an inheritance. But how much could he have gotten? He was paying Scott well. Sara wanted Scott to find out more, but he said it wasn't any of his business. It nagged at her. And the more she thought about it, the more awake she became. She remembered lunch after church one Sunday. Bill told them a little about Amber, but still he wasn't telling everything. Bill never talked about family, so who would have left him that kind of money? Sara couldn't let it go and she definitely couldn't sleep now.

She slipped out of bed to check on the kids. Shay was sound asleep, but Jeff was watching TV.

"You'd better get to sleep if you're going fishing tomorrow."

"I'll sleep when I'm dead."

She knew that was something he picked up from Scott.

"Get in that bed, boy," she told him as she turned off the TV. Jeff just lay on the floor staring at the dark screen. Sara couldn't believe how much he looked like his father. Even his mannerisms were the same. She wondered how that could be when he hadn't known his father but a few years before he died.

Sara walked back to the bedroom. As she got in bed, she heard Jeff lay down on the couch. Once she was sure everyone was settled, she finally drifted off to sleep.

21

The sport fisherman left the dock just as the sun was coming up. It looked as if it was going to be another perfect day for fishing. About a mile or so offshore, Jonas got all the lines in the water for a day of trolling. Jeff sat in the fighting chair from the time they left the dock.

As they began trolling, Bill asked Jeff if he had ever been fishing before.

"Not like this. Mostly in lakes and streams with my Uncle Mike. Do you think we'll catch anything?"

"More than likely, probably dolphin or wahoo. How old are you, Jeff?"

"Seventeen." Bill wondered what it would be like to be seventeen again and know what he knew now.

"Do you play any sports?"

"Not in school, but I'm on a paintball team."

"Paintball. That's different."

One of the reels began to sing. Jonas jumped into action. He set the hook and stuck the pole into the socket on the fighting chair. Scott got alongside Jeff and began coaching him.

"Wind in hard. Pull back. Wind in hard and let the pole move forward," he yelled as Jonas started reeling in the other lines. The fish jumped out of the water. It was a good-sized wahoo. Jeff was winding and pumping the rod. His feet were braced against the bottom of the chair. The Captain was busy keeping the boat on course. Bill took in the whole scene. This would be something to remember and he grabbed his camera. After about ten minutes, Jeff got the fish up to the boat, close enough for Jonas to gaff it.

Scott had never seen Jeff so proud or excited. The fish was over four feet long. Everybody was smiling and patting each other on the back. Jonas put the fish in the well cooler and started getting the lines back in the water. Jeff went to the cooler several times to look at his fish.

"That's the biggest fish I've ever seen! Wait 'til Uncle Mike sees this! He won't believe it." Jeff could hardly contain himself.

The Captain idled the boat alongside a weed line. Jonas brought in all the lines and got out some light spinning poles. Under the weed line were dolphin—not big, bullnose dolphin, but small one- to two-footers. On the light tackle, the fish felt like monsters and they would almost hit an empty hook. The men caught about fifteen keepers and let the small ones go.

"Hey Jonas, why don't you come relieve me for a while," the Captain yelled down from the high bridge.

They switched places. The Captain peed over the side of the boat and started putting lines out. Bill lent a hand. He was starting to catch on to the task. Jonas got the boat trolling again.

"I haven't done this in years, so you boys will have to help a little and bear with this old salt."

Scott and Bill pitched right in. Between the three men, they got all the hooks baited up and in the water. Jeff was back in the fighting chair.

"Bill, I thought about your offer and talked it over with that old woman of mine. She thinks it would be best. Otherwise, she said I'll just die if I don't have sum'thing to do. I think it's just to keep me out of her hair. Who knows? But anyway, you got a deal." The Captain handed Bill a sheet of paper. Bill studied it and asked, "You think this is fair enough?"

"Fair for everybody. It'll give me enough to live on and that's all I want. Well, that and to take care of my boat. If Jonas is involved, I won't have to worry about that."

"Good enough." They shook hands.

"Did you say anything to Jonas?" the Captain asked, looking up at the bridge.

There was Jonas, no shoes, cut off khaki pants, sleeveless tee shirt and sunglasses. He was black as the ace of spades and had one hand on the stainless steel wheel, scanning the ocean.

"No way. That's your job. It's your boat, Captain."

Bill went over and sat on the gunwale. He was anxious about spending so much money. If you never had money to spend and then started spending a bit, it would make anyone nervous. Bill pulled out his little book and scanned the numbers. Even after buying the condo, property and boat, he still hadn't spent his first million. Close, but no cigar. Also, he was still depositing money in the banks every day. It was gaining interest. That wasn't helping anything. Not that he wanted the money gone, he just had more than enough. Bill decided right then and there he had to start giving more of it away and he would need help with that. It would have to go where it would do the most good. *What a problem to have*, he thought as another fish hit his line.

***

The Captain never went back to the bridge. A good-sized marlin made an appearance while Jeff was in the chair, but as hard as he tried to land the fish, it got away. He talked about it all the way back to the dock.

Jonas came down from the bridge after all the tackle was brought in. The Captain told him not to worry about stowing it and to go ahead and take the boat back. Jonas was surprised. This was the first time the Captain let him do that. Jonas backed the boat into the slip perfectly.

Scott and Bill started unloading the cooler. Jeff pulled his fish out as a small crowd gathered around, admiring the catch.

Jonas winked at Scott and then hung Jeff's wahoo up for pictures. Jeff grabbed a rod and reel to pose with. He could see Sara and Shay coming up the dock. Scott began taking pictures with Bill's camera.

There was a lot of talking when Sara made her way through the crowd.

"Did you catch that, honey?" she asked.

Jeff couldn't say anything for the huge grin on his face.

"Well, tell her who caught that fish, honey," Bill said above the drone of the crowd. There were a few more chants of, "Yeah, honey," before Jeff could get out, "Me!"

Sara caught Scott's eyes. Neither of them could have been more proud or happy.

Jonas cleaned and filleted the fish. Bill and Scott helped the Captain stow the tackle and wash down the boat. Victoria came walking down the dock with her brothers. Both the boys had bright red tee shirts on with big, yellow letters that said, "Thing 1" and "Thing 2." Scott tapped Bill on the shoulder and pointed. Bill looked up and saw her and the boys. He smiled when their eyes met. This was all too perfect to be true. Something was going to have to go wrong. Then a thought entered his mind, *Put your trust in me.*

Where did that come from? Was God just talking to me?

As Bill greeted Victoria with a hug, Scott and Sara were taking pictures of Jeff and his fish, first by himself, then with Shay.

The Captain was taking in the whole scene. *I sure am going to miss this*, he thought. *At least I'll be able to go out when I feel like it instead of when I have to. Well, it's time to do this.* He walked towards Jonas.

"Good day, hey Captain?" Jonas said as he packed the last of the fish on ice. "Here, I almost forgot." Jonas reached in his pocket and pulled out the keys for the boat.

"Keep them, Jonas."

"What do you mean, Captain?" Jonas thought the Captain wanted him to have the keys as a memento of all the fishing he did on that boat.

"You'll need them. You're now part owner of the boat, along with me and Bill." Then the Captain added, "But you're going to do all the work."

"I'm confused. I thought you were retiring."

"I am. You're going to captain the boat. I'll just ride along once in a while. Don't let us down, Jonas."

Jonas was in shock. He slowly sat down and looked from the boat to the Captain. He couldn't believe it. He had gone from a drunk to a charter boat captain. God is great he thought.

Bill and Victoria could see the Captain and Jonas talking. When Jonas sat down on the cooler, Victoria looked at Bill with a concerned expression.

"Don't worry. Everything is okay," he said. "Give them a minute."

The old sea captain took off his hat, held it in his hand a moment looking it over, then put it on Jonas' head.

One of the men from the crowd walked up to Bill. "Who's the captain?" he asked. Bill pointed to Jonas and the Captain. "That black fellow sitting on the cooler." and then he added, "the one with the hat on."

"Thanks."

"Bill, what have you done?"

"You knew the Captain was retiring and he told me how hard it was going to be. Your dad made it one of the more successful boats around. Why shouldn't he captain it?"

"How can he?" Victoria asked and asked again, "What did you do?"

"Just slow down, pretty lady. All in due time."

Victoria started for Jonas as he sat on the cooler and began to cry. Thing One and Thing Two beat her there and began hugging him and climbing into his lap.

"Are you okay, Daddy? Are you hurt somewhere?" Thing Two asked when he saw the tears.

"Never better." He wiped away the tears of joy and stood up, one boy in each arm.

Victoria put her arm around Jonas' waist as the man from the crowd asked, "Excuse me, sir, but if you're not booked tomorrow I'd like to charter your boat. Maybe we can catch fish like you did today."

At first Jonas thought the man was talking to the Captain, but then he realized the fellow was looking at him. Jonas had never had a white man call him sir before.

"I don't fish on the Lord's Day, but I think I'm open Monday," Jonas told the man and looked at the Captain. The old salt nodded at Jonas.

"Monday it is then. There'll be five of us."

"All day or half?"

"All day."

"Good. Nine hundred for a full day. Be here at 6:30. One thing: this is a non-alcoholic boat."

"That's good, because I'll have my sons with me. We'll be here and no beer and such."

The Captain watched Jonas conduct his business. As the old salt slipped away towards home, he knew the boat was in good hands.

22

Elizabeth had a big meal ready as everybody came back from the dock. She was prepared to hear all the big fish stories. Sara and Victoria had helped set up the big table outside and string up the lights. It was another perfect night in paradise.

Victoria grilled some of the fresh fish with Bill at her side. Sara served food from the kitchen to the table. Shay and the boys played ball in the yard. Scott and Jonas stood together, both lost in their own thoughts.

Dinner was on the table and they all gathered round as Jonas rose to say the blessing.

"Dear Lord, thank you for what you have bestowed on this family. Thank you for your generosity. Thank you for our friends gathered around this table. But most of all, thank you for Jesus and taking away our sins. Please be with the Captain and bless this food. Amen."

Elizabeth leaned over and asked Jonas, "Is there something wrong with the Captain?"

"No, Mom, but I'm glad you're sitting down. You know he's retiring." Jonas could hardly contain himself as he blurted out, "I am now 1/3 owner of the Grand Illusion."

Everyone stopped eating and looked to Jonas. Elizabeth leaned back in her chair and began to fan herself. She couldn't catch her breath.

"Breathe, Mama, breathe. It's true," Victoria told her. Everybody was looking at Elizabeth when she finally sucked in a big gulp of air.

"Jonas, how can this be?" she asked.

"Only by the power of God."

"Praise God," she shouted and everybody said, "Amen."

"Well, let's see if God can help you now," an unknown voice shouted.

It was Pop Pop coming out of the shadows with a gun pointed at Victoria.

"If she don't want me then no one can have her and you're next, white boy." He began to squeeze the trigger.

Scott brought the aluminum baseball bat down so hard on Pop Pop's wrist that it shattered bones up his arm. From the tinny sound of the aluminum bat, Scott assumed he'd hit a home run.

Pop Pop let out a scream of pain that was heard across the island. Scott picked up the cheap pistol and put it in his pocket. He then smacked Pop Pop in the head and knocked him out. Everyone at the table watched in disbelief. Scott casually walked to the table, sat down and began to eat. "Nice friends you got there, Jonas. Could you pass the fish, please?"

Thing One and Two jumped up from the table and ran to Pop Pop. They began poking him with their feet.

"You think he's dead?" Thing One asked Two.

"I don't know. I ain't never seen a dead person before."

Bill looked at Scott calmly eating dinner and began to laugh. Then Jeff started and pretty soon everyone was laughing except Scott. He just kept eating as if what had just happened was an everyday thing. Then finally Scott joined in and began laughing at the absurdity of the situation.

***

Bill threw a bucket of cold water on the now-bound Pop Pop. He came to and looked around. He didn't like what he saw. Bill, Jonas and Scott stood over him in the boat. Scott said, "Bobby, I'm going to troll for sharks and you're going to be the bait." Jonas waved the largest hook anyone had seen in front of the bound man's face.

"Should I hook him through the neck or up his butt?" Jonas asked. Pop Pop was starting to get the picture as Bill poured more bloody chum into the water. "Through the neck, but don't hit that big vein. We want him to struggle. It'll attract the really big ones," Scott told Jonas.

Pop Pop pissed in his pants and passed out. All the men laughed.

"Take us in, Jonas. I think he got the message. Did you get all that on tape, Jeff?" Bill asked, smiling at Scott.

"Sure did and the only face on tape is his."

Pop Pop woke up on the beach covered in sand, still bound. A cassette tape was shoved in his mouth with duct tape across it. Grand Cayman Island isn't that big, but neither Jonas nor his family ever heard from Pop Pop again.

***

Nobody wanted to leave, but Sara, Scott and their kids were the first. Bill stayed a few extra days.

Bill had Sara go with him to pick out a ring for Victoria. It wasn't the biggest one around, but it was the most beautiful one. He still hadn't asked Victoria the magic question and he was anxious to do so.

On Bill's last night on the island, he and Victoria went out to eat. Alone. This was their first date without an escort of any kind and it was a nice change. Bill suggested they walk up the beach to wear off some of the food they had just eaten. It wasn't a ploy. He just wanted to spend as much time with her as possible knowing that he had to leave in the morning. It was another warm, pretty night with a large thunderstorm to the east lighting up the sky. As they walked along the shore, neither spoke until Bill broke the silence.

"Victoria, can I ask you something?"

She was sure it was going to be about the Pop Pop incident, but she didn't want to talk about it. "I guess, as long as it's not about Pop Pop."

"It isn't," he said as he turned to her. "Will you spend the rest of your life with me?" He opened up his hand to reveal the ring.

Victoria's eyes lit up as she stuck out her slender hand. It didn't take her long to answer.

"Yes, forever," Bill slipped the ring on her finger.

Bill left the next morning. He promised to be back in three weeks, but he knew it would feel like an eternity to him and Victoria.

23

Everybody had a lot to do—Elizabeth and Victoria had a wedding to plan. Jonas had a new business to run. Scott had a house to build. Bill had money to deposit and give away.

Elizabeth and Victoria started making plans right away. They set a date and started looking for a dress. After a long debate about whether the wedding should be outside or indoors, the two of them finally agreed on an outdoor wedding. They had plenty of time to plan for the big day, but Elizabeth felt pressured because there was so much to do.

Jonas gladly went fishing every day. Each morning before pulling away from the dock, he made sure to thank God for his good fortune. Bill had convinced him to set up a website and Jonas had to turn away business because there were so many people who were interested in a fishing trip with him. The Captain had gone out on several trips, finally allowing himself to relax and enjoy fishing instead of worrying about everyone else. Jonas's new mate was a young, white boy who lived only with his mother—his father had been killed during England's short war with Argentina.

Jonas knew the two of them struggled. The boy had no interest in school, but he always volunteered at church when he was able and he had some experience fishing, so Jonas enjoyed his company.

Even though Jonas now owned a computer, he still preferred to do his books by hand. His journal was perfect, every nickel and dime accounted for. He was making money for himself and his partners and fishing every day wasn't a bad way to make a living. The boat was kept in shipshape and he and the young mate got along just fine.

Elizabeth, Victoria, Jonas and the boys were having the time of their lives. There was never a moment that went by when one of them wasn't thanking God for what He had done.

***

Scott and Bill had their hands full. Building a house was hard enough, but with Bill missing Victoria, winter coming on and Fred's laziness, things were a bit overwhelming. Nothing ever really bothered Scott, but when he sensed Bill getting bound up he would say, "Yo Bill. When the going gets tough, the tough go riding." They would pack up their tools and spend the rest of the day cruising on the parkway.

Fred, on the other hand, was a different sort of bird. He was Scott's best friend which meant that no matter what he did or said, Scott always overlooked his faults. Sara didn't quite fall on the same page—she swore he had mental problems, but Scott knew more about him than she did and understood why he acted in the way that he did. It's funny what people will do to protect themselves.

Bill didn't know how to handle Fred half the time, even though they had known each other a while. Fred had been married twice and had two kids with his first wife. He cheated on both more than you could count. He had declared bankruptcy once and he still lived with his mother. The only job he could hold was with Scott, because Scott was the only one who could really tolerate him.

Bill would send Fred to Home Depot and he would come back with only half the materials on the list. Bill would ask if he had checked the list, only to find out Fred had lost it before he got to the store. Scott could see when Bill was getting frustrated and would step in to calm things down. Scott and Fred had worked together so long that each of them knew what to expect from the other. Scott also knew enough to respect Fred, because regardless of his shortcomings, he was still a man who could be depended on when the chips were down.

One cold, crisp, winter morning, Scott and Bill were drinking coffee, waiting on Fred. Scott decided he would try and explain how things were with Fred. The day before Bill had gotten pretty frustrated with him.

"You know, Bill, Fred's a little different, but he's a good guy."

"I know what you're saying, but sometimes I just expect more from him."

"I've learned to overlook a lot of things. If I could get him to attend church regularly, I think he would stop drinking so much. I don't think I'm making excuses for him, but everyone has their own demon they have to wrestle, you know? I love Fred like a brother, but sometimes I could kick his ass. You just have to learn to bear with him." Scott felt like he had said enough and hoped Bill understood.

Bill looked at Scott and said, "He told me you used to drink a lot and smoke a little or maybe it was the other way around."

"Well, he talks too much," Scott smiled and reluctantly answered, "I did until I realized it was abusing me." Scott paused and looked away before continuing. "My mother always had a problem with booze and I didn't want to end up like that. Besides, when Sara and I got together there was no way she was going to put up with that... but I do miss the smoke every now and then."

"Yea, I know what you mean." Both of them pondered in silence until Bill interrupted, "Well, Fred told me a lot more and let me just say that I'm glad we're friends, 'cause I'd hate to be your enemy." The Pop Pop incident came to Bill's mind.

"Since I met Sara and have been in church, I'm not like that anymore." At least that's what Scott hoped everybody thought. It's hard to change the stripes on a tiger.

"Just the same, I'd rather be your friend. We are friends, aren't we?" Bill asked Scott.

Scott took a sip of coffee and looked long and hard at Bill.

"You know, Bill, I count most of my friends on one hand. That includes the dead ones. A friend to me is someone I can call anytime or for any reason. They always have your back and wouldn't say anything about you they wouldn't say to your face. Fred's my friend and so is big Todd from church."

Bill nodded. "The big Sunday school teacher?"

"You can say it-the fat guy?" They both chuckled. "Yeah, him." He really was fat, weighing over 450 pounds. "I know I can depend on the two of them and that's about it."

"You think you can depend on Fred? Hell, he can't even go to the store without screwing it up."

"Believe me, Bill, he'll come through in a pinch. When I started dating Sara and going to church, 'friends' fell by the wayside. There weren't many to begin with, but Fred was always there."

"Yeah, I know what you mean. He made sure to consistently check on me after Amber was killed." Scott knew he had crossed a bridge with Bill when he mentioned Amber. "Anyway, where does that leave me?" Bill tried to change the subject, knowing that Scott was still thinking about what he had just said.

"We're getting there, Bill. Slowly," Scott answered, pouring himself another cup of coffee.

"I never had a chance to thank you for what you did at Jonas' house that night. I've never seen someone move that fast. Fred told me of your training in the service."

"You're welcome. Again, sometimes Fred just talks too much. Let's just leave it at that."

Scott looked out the window as Fred drove up. Good timing, Freddy.

"Let's go to work," Scott said as he smiled at Bill.

Bill smiled back, but thought about how almost everybody he knew was damaged goods. Even the people who seem put together on the outside, have been torn apart in some form or fashion. It was comforting to know he wasn't alone in his pain.

***

The house was coming along. All the logs were in place and, fortunately, the roof was on because the weather was turning cold. It would be especially cold on top of the mountain because of elevation and exposure.

Bill continued to attend church with Scott and Sara. He joined Todd's Sunday school class and volunteered for different activities and events around the church. He wanted to be on the security team with Scott, but without any experience he was afraid to ask. Bill would help at youth functions by cooking meals and cleaning up. He would notice one of the security team members at every function the church held. They were very low key and rarely had to step into a situation. Most of them were local law enforcement officers. The church was large enough to have a paid deputy on hand for Sunday and Wednesday night services. Bill wondered how they liked taking orders from Scott, as he had no law enforcement training. One Sunday morning, he got a chance to ask. The answer was unexpected.

Bill was standing next to an older gentleman waiting to enter the sanctuary when Scott walked up. Only then did Bill notice the ear buds in both men's ears. All security team personnel carried two way radios.

Scott spoke to the man, saying something about patrolling this service. Scott nodded to Bill and asked, "Hey man, how'd you like Sunday school?"

"It was great. Todd is so real, like one of us."

"Yeah, he is," replied Scott as he looked at the man standing beside Bill. "Ah, Bill, this is Clarence. He helps with the security."

Clarence stuck out his hand. "Nice to meet you. I'm Clarence Hill."

"Good to meet you. Scott has spoken about you several times."

Clarence was retired from the State Patrol. Although soft-spoken he had a reputation for being very tough.

Bill asked, "You're not the same trooper who patrols around here, are you?"

"I used to work this area."

"You gents will have to excuse me. I've got to get the preacher," and Scott left in a hurry.

Bill turned to Clarence. "I actually think I've met you before, then. I think you investigated an accident I had. A drunk ran into me as I was getting off the Naples exit. You had your hands full with him."

Clarence remembered and the conversation continued as one thing led to another.

"Clarence, let me ask you one question. You know Scott and I work together and I know he doesn't have any law enforcement background. In fact, he's been on the other side a few times. So what's it like having him run the security team?"

Clarence thought for a moment. "We all respect him. He makes good decisions. I believe he would always be there if any of us needed anything." With that, Clarence turned and went into the sanctuary.

This wasn't the first time someone had asked this question. Clarence knew Scott had been on the other side of his employment and never been caught. He also knew Scott had been in tight situations and was lucky to be alive. Each had earned the other's respect.

That Sunday, Pastor Carol reminded the congregation that giving was part of God's command. He wasn't just talking about a tithe of ten percent, but also giving of yourself to others. As Bill sat next to Sara in the pew, he finally began to understand.

Bill left the next day for the Caymans to spend a few days with Victoria. Scott and Fred continued work on the house. Things were settling down into a nice routine, but Scott wondered about what kind of work he would have when the house was finished. There was some outside work to be done that would only take them until the end of spring to complete.

Bill and Victoria planned for a March wedding before Easter because the weather in the Caymans wouldn't be too hot. Bill's parents were no longer living and he was an only child so there weren't many relatives. Bill's list of guests for the wedding was short. He would ask Scott to be his best man and Fred and one of Vic's cousins to be his groomsman.

Victoria, on the other hand, was inviting half the island. Bill loved it, though. He never saw her so happy.

Jonas' house was abuzz, women coming and going all day, every day. Jonas was glad to be fishing. He had given all his odd jobs to a man who went to church with him. This let Jonas concentrate on his charters. He was fast becoming a name around the docks. If you wanted to fish and catch fish, not party, his was the boat you wanted.

Bill and Victoria loved to sit on a bench at the docks and talk for hours. Finally the question Bill dreaded came up.

"Bill, Daddy has asked me several times what you do for a living. Can you support me?" She hesitated. "I want to know, too." She looked at him with those big, brown eyes and he didn't want to lie to her, but what could he do?

Bill thought for a moment and said, "I inherited a bunch of money and… I got lucky because I invested it well." And he had.

There. That wasn't a lie exactly. He did "inherit" the money. It was almost the perfect crime, stealing from the guys who stole it in the first place. Bill hadn't left many clues.

Sure, the FBI had left no stone unturned, but Bill looked clean. When Agent Bishop looked at Bill's bank account there was very little money in it. The other two accounts Bill had opened up were under false names. The Cayman accounts were unknown to the FBI.

The only major transaction Bishop could find was for the property. That was a cash purchase and not enough to set off any bells. It wasn't so large that Bill couldn't have saved the money. Bishop also knew Bill had been fired from his job and applied for unemployment. Bishop didn't think someone with millions of dollars would do that.

Bishop keyed in on the three suspects he had in jail. Each one had turned against the other and they were accusing each other of getting all the money. It was a puzzling situation, although there have been stranger and far more puzzling ones. Bishop knew that given enough time he would figure this one out.

The FBI knew more about Bill than he liked. They knew about Amber. After searching Bill's warehouse, they knew he had been living there, at least sleeping there, but it wasn't something they reported to the manager.

Of course, Bill didn't know how close the FBI looked at him and the inheritance story seemed to fly with Scott and Sara.

"How much is a bunch?" Victoria asked Bill.

Bill stared at her and then said, "Come on. I'll show you."

They drove to Bill's condo. In a locked closet were shelves piled with stacks of hundred dollar notes. There were also several handguns and ammunition.

"Don't say anything yet. Let's go to the bank," Bill said.

Victoria had never seen that much cash in her whole life. Even if she put together all her family had ever made at one time, it would never have equaled a tenth of what was in the closet.

At the bank, a man greeted Bill as if he knew him. Bill handed him a small paper bag. The banker ushered them into his plush office. A young lady dressed smartly entered to see if they would like something to drink. Victoria was amazed. The tellers hardly spoke to her at the windows and she had always felt out of place in the bank.

"This is a pleasant surprise, Mr. August. How can we help you today?" the banker asked in his proper British accent as he eyed Victoria.

"This is my bride-to-be and I want to disclose to her what 'we' have in your bank." Bill stressed the "we." Without question or hesitation, the man typed some numbers into his desktop computer. He spun the screen around for Victoria to see. She fell back into her chair.

Bill had been a busy little bee on his trips to see her, accumulating over $1 million in this bank alone. Bill pulled out his small journal and compared numbers. Taking into account the interest, they matched.

"I would like to transfer $50,000 into Victoria's account. Also, I need to make a donation to a church in North Carolina, anonymously, of course. Here is the contact info. Can you take care of that please?"

"Not a problem. You know we will be very discreet."

"Thanks," Bill got up to leave. Victoria was still deep in her seat. Bill helped her up.

Outside Bill told her she could ask any question of him she liked.

"How much are you worth, altogether?" she asked rather sheepishly, but Bill could tell she meant business.

"Almost fifteen and a half in cash, plus my investments," He didn't want to say the million part, not liking the way it sounded, like he was bragging.

"I need to sit down," Victoria said as she grabbed onto Bill's arm. They found a bench under a crop of palm trees.

"I can't imagine that much money." Victoria paused. "And why did you put money in my account?"

"I want you to have the most perfect wedding you can think of…or you can give it all away. I trust you. You'll figure it out."

They sat for a while, then Victoria spoke. "I'm glad you never told me about the money before I fell in love with you. You won't mind if I give it away, will you?"

"No, no. Do with it what you think is best. I just don't want you to worry about money again, ever. I'm going to set up a trust account for your brothers so they can go to school or whatever. And your dad, well hell. He seems to be having the time of his life."

Victoria couldn't believe this man. Money hadn't corrupted him. He wasn't greedy and didn't need more. There weren't any airs about him. He was just Bill and she loved him with her whole being. She snuggled up closer to him on the bench and put her arms around him.

"Please, Victoria, don't tell anyone. I would hate for anyone to know about the money. People act different when they find out how rich someone is and I want everyone to be themselves around me."

"Don't worry. Your secret is safe with me. No one would believe me anyway."

They got back to Victoria's house in time to see the charter boats dock. It was obvious that Jonas had a good day.

24

By the time Bill returned to North Carolina, Scott had heard about the large donation to the church. No one knew who the donor was and no one was confessing. That was kind of strange for a church.

Scott was hoping to get some money to purchase extra cameras for the security system. Throughout the church there were cameras positioned in critical areas, in the sanctuary, nursery and the hallways. But Scott needed a few more for blind areas. The cameras were monitored in the security room during the services.

There had been a few incidents since 9/11, but nothing major. Scott held meetings once every month to update the team. He would go over new policies or procedures and allow the men to fellowship with each other. Scott knew all off-duty law enforcement officers carried concealed weapons. They, the law dogs, frowned on civilians who carried one. Scott tactfully avoided the issue, but on his ankle and in the middle of his lower back he could feel the weight of his weapons.

By Christmas, the house was almost complete. Bill planned to spend the holidays with Victoria. He gave Scott and Fred time off from December 20th to the second week in January, with pay, of course.

Bill stayed an extra two weeks. Scott and Fred joked that he couldn't pull himself away.

"Could you?" asked Fred.

"Why, hell no," Scott replied.

The two men were up at Bill's putting in walkways and landscaping. They were also getting ready to move the cabin, which they now referred to as the guest house.

"What's the age difference between them?" Fred asked.

"Let's see, she's 22, I think and Bill's…" Scott trailed off doing the math. "Twelve years, maybe. Me and Sara are nine years."

"Nothing like younger women."

Scott thought of a Jimmy Buffett song after Fred's comment.

"What's hard to believe is he's gonna marry a nigger."

Scott bristled and flashed an angry look at Fred. "You know I hate that word. Besides, you'd marry her in a heartbeat to get in her pants."

"Sorry and you're right, except I'd only promise to marry her." They both laughed. "What's her family like?"

Scott smiled as he thought of the time spent with them. "Pretty tight. Jonas, her father, is fun to be around. He's been around the block once or twice. Very religious."

"Great, another Bible thumper. Just what I need."

"No, what you need is AA and some church. You need a whole lot of church. You know, when we go down there for the wedding, you won't be able to drink."

"What, is my throat going to close up when we get there or something? Besides, I don't drink that much. I can stop anytime."

"Spoken like a true drunk. You sound just like my mom. That crap has started pickling your brain. You're going to end up under a bridge somewhere." Scott stopped. Fred was a man and he wouldn't lecture him.

"Just as long as I have my bottle of Crown Royal."

"Bridge dwellers drink MD 20-20."

"That'll be all right, too." They both laughed again. "Besides, I've always got you, right, honey?" and they laughed harder.

***

Bill got in late Saturday night but still got up early enough to get to church the next morning. The preacher was at the back door greeting people when Bill arrived. They shook hands and Carol commented on Bill's nice tan.

"I'm seeing a girl who lives in the Caymans. Well, I'm doing more than seeing her. We're going to get married in two months," Bill told him.

"Congratulations! I can't wait to meet her," Preacher Carol replied. "Can you come up to my office after the service? I'd like to talk to you."

"Sure thing, Preacher," Bill answered, assuming he was going to talk to him about marriage.

***

Scott escorted the preacher to his office on the third floor after the service. A deputy was standing guard at the office door. Scott had the deputy sweep the office after every service before the preacher went in.

"He's going to be awhile. Someone is coming up to talk to him. I'll get him to his car," Scott told the deputy.

"Thanks, man," The deputy handed his radio to Scott. "Could you put this up for me?"

"No problem."

The deputy passed Bill in the hallway and they nodded to each other. The deputy looked back at Scott, who gave the thumbs up sign.

"Hey Scott, is it okay to go in?"

"Sure man, he's expecting you," Scott assumed a position beside the door.

Bill went through a small outer office into the preacher's large but cluttered office.

"Hey Bill. Take a seat." Bill was surprised the preacher knew his name. With over 2,000 members how could he remember everyone's name?

Bill sat on a loveseat with a small table in front of it. The preacher sat on the couch.

"So you're going to get married?" the preacher asked.

"Yes sir."

"And you say you met her in the Caymans?"

"Yep. She was born there. A native, I guess you could say. I think her parents were born there, too," Bill told him, not wanting to go into great detail. He was feeling a little uncomfortable when the preacher got up and shut the door.

"Is she a Christian girl?"

"She is and so is her whole family," Bill said proudly.

"So where does that leave you?"

Bill wasn't expecting that question. He thought carefully for a moment and said, "I've got some things in my past that I've done which keep haunting me. Every time you open up the invitation I get ready to come down and this little voice says to me, 'What if somebody finds out the things you've done?' and it stops me."

"We've all got things in our past we're not proud of. Look at Todd and Scott. Once you put your trust in Jesus, he takes away all that sin. You need to get past it and let God deal with it."

"It sounds so easy when you put it that way."

"It is easy, but I've got something else I want to ask you. Know that anything you say stays in this room and I do mean anything."

"I understand, but I'm more afraid of what you might ask or say than whether it leaves this room."

The preacher smiled and said, "The church has received two checks from a Cayman Bank for $250,000. You wouldn't know anything about that, would you?"

Bill hung his head. *Busted!*, he thought. "Yeah, that was me."

"Bill, where did you get that kind of money? The truth, please."

Bill thought long and hard for a few minutes. "I'm not willing to say right now, but I can assure you no one got hurt over it in any way. I'd like to say God dropped it in my lap, but I don't know." Bill hung his head even lower. "Can I still attend church here?"

Preacher Carol looked at Bill. He would rather have heard another answer, but this would have to do for now. Other pastors might say, "Don't look a gift horse in the mouth," but not Pastor Carol.

"I'll tell you what I'm going to do, Bill. We're going to deposit the money in a separate account and not use it. When the time comes and you feel you can tell me about it, then I'll decide if it's ok to keep it. Fair enough?"

Bill shook his head. "Sounds good to me. And believe me, I'm trying to figure it out."

"I'll keep praying for you, Bill. God will let you know what to do. Let's close with a word of prayer."

Preacher Carol prayed and Bill listened for answers.

Bill didn't go to the usual after-church lunch with Scott and Sara. He went right home and began to think about everything that happened or was happening. He also prayed. Later that evening he called Scott to get the preacher's phone number.

"Everything okay, Bill?" Scott asked. He was concerned. Scott could hear the stress in Bill's voice.

"Yes and no."

"Is there anything I can help you with? I mean, you're all right? I don't need to come up there or anything?"

"No, no. It's not like that. I'm fine."

Scott gave Bill the number and told Bill he'd see him in the morning.

Bill called the preacher. They exchanged hellos and how are you's.

"Carol, I'm ready to accept God into my life. Do I need to come to your house to pray?" Bill asked.

"No, no. We can pray over the phone."

Bill prayed the sinner's prayer over the phone with the preacher. After hanging up, Bill felt a peace come over him like never before. He knew now that God was truly in control, but there were still no answers to his questions.

***

Fred didn't come to work the next day. Bill was glad, because he wanted to talk to Scott about things.

"Scott, it's just you and me today. Fred called in. He has the flu," They both laughed. Scott had told Bill awhile back that Fred was a hypochondriac.

It was a beautiful, late winter day, not a cloud in the sky. The temperature was in the high thirties with no wind. It felt warmer. They were clearing brush and cutting wood today. It wasn't long before the heavy coats came off and sleeves rolled up. Standing at the brush fire drinking coffee at the morning break, Bill started.

"Scott, I need to tell you something."

Scott thought, *Here it comes. No more work.*

"I accepted Christ last night, but I still don't have any answers yet."

Scott smiled. "God doesn't work on your time table. He has his own. I'm truly happy for you. It's the best decision you'll ever make. I know it was for me."

"Yeah, thanks. Now if I can just forget about things I've done, I would be better."

"Believe me, Bill, there's nothing you've done that isn't forgiven. I know. Todd and I talked at length about that. I could tell you things that would make your head spin and it's all been forgiven. But I know what you mean about the guilt and all. You think, 'How can anyone forgive me for what I've done?' It's not anyone; it's God. Listen to me. I sound like a preacher. Todd would be proud."

Scott was relieved that Bill hadn't said anything about not working any more, but he surely was uncomfortable talking about God for two reasons. One, he wasn't that knowledgeable about God and salvation. And two, it didn't seem too macho for men to be standing around talking about God. Then, Scott thought about David in the Bible—you don't get much more macho than him. David was Scott's favorite person in the Bible. You couldn't screw up more than he did and, still, God forgave him.

"Have you told Jonas and Victoria yet?" Scott asked Bill as they started to put more brush on the fire.

"No, I didn't want to do it over the phone." Bill's mind flashed to Victoria. He could picture her standing in church. "That church service we attended with them was wild, wasn't it?"

"Ain't no doubt about that. I've never seen anything like it before. Sara and Shay said it was like that when they were in Africa. People danced, sang, clapped and shouted. Sometimes I wish Piney Branch would get like that, but no, white people are too reserved. Well, with Easter coming maybe the preacher will get them wound up." He stopped to look at Bill. "Let me ask you something."

Bill was nervous. "Go ahead."

"Well, Victoria's black. What do you think about that? I was just wondering. You know, living in the South and all."

Bill thought that was a strange question coming from Scott. Bill knew that on Martin Luther King Day Scott made Fred listen to a CD of speeches King made and Scott hated the "N" word. He even explained how hard it was for him to overcome his prejudices.

"I thought you weren't prejudiced. At least, that's what you said."

"Hell, I'm not, except against blacks, Mexicans, women and cripples."

Bill's mouth dropped open and Scott began to roar with laughter.

Bill understood Scott's sarcasm and began to explain after they stopped laughing. "When I first met Jonas, I felt a peace around him. That's one reason I like being around him. Also, he never asked me for anything. It felt good to be around him. Peaceful, no tension. When he sent Victoria to pick me up that evening, it was the same feeling, only much stronger. With her, I knew it was love at first sight. She is the most beautiful woman I've ever seen, but the peace that surrounds her made her much more than pretty. You get what I'm saying? It's hard to explain."

"I get it. I'm not totally insensitive." Scott paused, then came the real question.

"One more thing, Bill. Where in the hell did you really get all this money you spend?"

The question caught Bill off guard and he stumbled speaking at first. "I…I…oh…ah." Bill cleared his throat and said, "I promise I will tell you someday, just not today. You won't believe me anyway."

Scott let it drop. "Now tell me, Scott, is everything they say about you true?"

Scott looked up at Bill. No words were spoken. From the look on Scott's face none were needed. Bill got the picture.

"Most of it," Scott said in a low growl.

"Well, I'm glad you're my friend. We are friends now, aren't we?"

"I guess so, but that doesn't mean I'm going to share my wife with you," and both men chuckled.

"Scott, that day in the boat with Pop Pop," Scott stopped dragging brush and looked up in the sky. "Would you have thrown him overboard if Jonas hadn't stopped you?"

"He should have let me. I don't like looking over my shoulder all the time. I have to do that enough. If he ain't around, that would be one less worry."

"I'm real glad you're my friend," Bill smiled, trying to break the tension.

Fred must have been really sick, because he didn't show up for the next two days. This gave Scott and Bill time to work a lot of things out. It snowed and then snowed some more. Bill was forced to park his truck at the bottom of the mountain and use an ATV to go up to the house. After the first snow, instead of working on the house, the guys went to Scott's to work on their bikes.

Scott told Bill about meeting Sara, about her two children and personal things, never more than one or two things at once. Slowly Bill was getting the whole story, one piece at a time.

On Saturdays they would all go four wheeling or ride ATV's. Some people from the church would come over. Scott would build a big fire. While the kids rode, everyone else would try to stay warm around the fire and drink hot chocolate.

Everybody would kid Bill about missing Victoria. Fred and Scott were particularly hard on Bill. What were friends for?

"Don't worry, Bill. I'm sure Jody's taking good care of her and spending your money doing it."

"Scott, that's not what I need to hear right now. Sometimes you're a real butthole."

"What do you mean sometimes?" Sara chipped in.

Bill would slip off and call Victoria on the spur of the moment. Every now and then Bill would tell Scott, "Handle things. I'm going to be gone for a few days."

Scott knew where he was going. Bill would be gone more and more as the wedding grew closer.

Soon enough, the wedding was only a week away. People packed, made plans, loaded up and made their way to Grand Cayman.

Due to the distance and expense, not a lot of people associated with Bill made the trip: Scott and his family, Fred (by himself), Todd and a few others made sure they were there. Victoria, on the other hand, invited everybody.

Scott and Fred had a bet that Fred wouldn't drink from when they left to when they got back. Fred was determined to win. On the plane Scott had the steward deliver a drink to Fred, which promptly got him the one-finger salute from Fred.

The wedding went off without a hitch. Sara told Scott that Victoria was planning on moving back to North Carolina with Bill. This worried Sara because she wasn't sure if Scott had completed Bill's home or not. Fred kept saying they still had a lot to do, only because he wanted to keep working, he needed the income.

Fred kept hitting on Victoria's friends to no avail, but he wasn't drinking. Jonas tried to witness to Fred which was a losing cause, but he never gave up.

The small church was crowded. Every seat on the bride's side was filled. Some even sat on Bill's side. The inside of the church was modestly decorated, white flowers and some greenery. The wedding party was small: Bill, of course and Scott, Fred and one of Victoria's cousins.

When Victoria entered from the rear of the sanctuary, everyone rose. Her long brown hair was curled and twisted with small white flowers in a ring around the top of her head. The white, silk dress was sleeveless and came to the top of her feet, its whiteness contrasting with her bronze skin. Everything about her was simple, but elegant. The crowd let out a collective sigh as they all marveled at her beauty. Even Scott, "Mr. Cool," wavered. He poked Bill and whispered, "Already had her."

Bill turned and said, "Yeah, Sara told me last night."

Both smiled at the locker room humor. Jonas was a basket case, tears streaming down his face. Her two brothers shared the job of the ring bearer.

The service was simple. There was no singing, lighting of candles, or pouring of sand. Nothing but the preacher reading from the Bible and the reciting of the vows. When he said, "You may kiss the bride," Bill was nervous. After all, Jonas was watching, but when their lips met, it was as if they were alone. The room swirled and Bill thought he would lose his balance. It wasn't until Scott said, "Okay, okay. Get a room," that they broke off and the crowd cheered and clapped. There wouldn't be a receiving line with awkward introductions.

Everybody returned to Jonas' for the reception. A large tent had been erected in the yard with an army of caterers waiting on the guests. All local food was served, jerk chicken and pork, rice and beans, fish and fruit. A calypso band and a reggae band rotated in and out, so there was always music.

Elizabeth was beside herself playing hostess. She moved from table to table speaking with everyone. Jonas made sure to always sit near Fred, trying to witness to him. Bill and Victoria changed into casual clothing after the pictures.

The party continued well into the night with everybody having a good time, dancing, eating and kids running around everywhere. Scott sat by himself at one of the four long tables tensely watching the people and the party. Jonas was talking to Fred, the Captain was telling fishing stories to several men and a group of women were gossiping about Victoria's white dress. What struck Scott as funny was how white some of the people were and how black others were, but no one cared. They were all just people and friends.

"Penny for your thoughts?" asked Sara as she walked up to him.

"Hell, they ain't worth that," Scott said.

"Well, try me." She thought for a moment about how everything had worked out. She was having a good time and, for a change, not worrying about anything. "So what's on that mind?"

Scott looked around and in a twist of Rodney King's words said, "I guess we all *can* get along... for now anyway." He smiled up at Sara, but deep down he had a feeling that God had bigger plans for him.

The big decision for Bill was the honeymoon. Where do you go when you're already living in paradise? He decided on Key West and from there they would fly to Orlando. Once there they would meet Jonas, Elizabeth and the boys and take in the theme parks. Jonas protested, but Bill insisted once again.

From Florida, Bill would rent a car and the whole family would slowly drive to North Carolina. Bill felt like Jonas should know where his daughter was going to live. He also wanted him to visit his church.

Bill and Victoria left on schedule and the party continued until a little after midnight. Not a negative word could be said about the whole affair.

Everyone spent the next day recuperating, but once they were rested, all the men went fishing with Jonas. Big Todd and Jonas talked Bible all day, which gave Fred a break. Jeff caught the biggest fish again. Scott was proud, even though Jeff rubbed it in at every chance. The girls lay on the beach until it got too hot, then went shopping.

Everyone missed Bill and Victoria. Fred had given Bill a video camera as a wedding gift. He made sure to tell him it was for the wedding night, but that was just Fred. No harm done.

Everyone made it home, safe, tired and tanned.

25

Jonas attended church with Bill and Victoria. Sara planned a small reception in the hospitality room of the church. They had coffee and cake after the second service. Todd and Jonas had became quick friends. Todd promised to visit often, saying in his loud, deep voice, "The Bible and fishing. How much better can it get? Praise God!"

Preacher Carol told Jonas, "It's too bad you can't be here for Easter next week. We always have a special service."

"Thank you for the invitation, but I need to get back. I've got several charters planned and it'll be busy all week with spring break coming on," Jonas explained.

Todd came up and patted Jonas on the back. "Jonas here is a self-taught Bible scholar, Carol. You should talk to him sometime about it."

Jonas blushed, knowing the preacher had a doctorate in divinity.

The big question for Victoria was how she liked North Carolina and Bill's house.

Her answer was always the same. "When Bill said his house was remote he wasn't kidding, but as long as he's there I'm okay. Besides, we've got the condo by Dad's when I get homesick."

"Anytime you get lonely just call and we'll get together," Sara told Victoria, putting her hand on Victoria's arm.

Then Fred spoke up. "Don't worry, Sara. I won't let her get lonely. She can call me anytime."

"Fred, you're full of it. I can smell you from here," Bill said from the end of the table.

"Sara, you need to take her shopping soon. There're a few items we need for the house and she needs some warmer clothes. Maybe tomorrow?" Bill asked.

"Sounds good to me. I'll ask my mom to come."

Victoria didn't know how to take Fred and after she and Bill left the church she asked, "What did Fred mean by not letting me get lonely?"

"He thinks all women want him. It was just a joke, Vic," Bill explained.

"Bill, we pledged ourselves to each other in front of God. I would never do anything to break that, no matter what."

"I know. Don't worry, It's just men talking, no big deal."!

"Did Sara leave her husband? I heard someone say Scott had adopted her children."

"No, he left her. He passed away when the children were young."

"Oh. I don't want to think anything like that. I couldn't…" and Victoria trailed off.

"We do what we have to do and keep going."

"I love you so much I wouldn't want to go on. Let's not talk about it."

"Vic, you never know what God's got planned, but I'm not worried."

The rest of the week flew by. The guys worked up at Bill's house and Victoria and Sara shopped and cleaned every day.

Bill hadn't done much decorating—he decided to leave that job for Victoria. After all, it was her home, too. It really helped Victoria having Sara around. The separation from her family was hard. At least having something to do, like all the things they needed for the house, filled her time.

They all planned to attend Easter service together. Scott and Bill even talked Fred into attending.

26

Scott got to church early Easter Sunday morning. He had a lot to do. Easter Sunday was always the largest service of the year. People who didn't attend all year would come on Easter Sunday or Christmas. Fathers who wouldn't attend with their families would make an exception for today. Some families brought relatives who went to other churches so they could all be together.

Scott assembled all the security volunteers together and gave a small pep talk. He had four men patrolling around the church. There was one paid deputy on duty, as usual. His main job would be escorting the offering to the safe, along with the head usher and one security team member.

Scott would escort the preacher from his office to the pulpit. They had predetermined signals the preacher would use if he felt threatened or wanted the security men closer. Also, on either side of the stage were small electronic signs which displayed numbers. It was for the nursery in case your child was having a problem. The security team had numbers known only to them. These coded numbers meant things such as a fire or medical emergency.

Scott left the security room and headed to the third floor. The church halls were already crowded. He stood outside the preacher's door waiting for him.

"Morning Preacher," Scott said, shaking his hand. "Going to have a big crowd today."

"Good morning Scott. It's too bad they don't come all the time, not just once or twice a year," Carol replied.

"Where we headed this morning?"

"Front entrance." The two men headed for the front of the church with Scott in the lead. On the way down Scott spoke into the small microphone clipped to his shirt.

"Okay guys, we're on the way down, heading to the front entrance."

All of the security team personnel had two-way radios. So did the one man in the security room. He monitored four TV screens which were connected to cameras in and about of the church.

Preacher Carol shook hands and spoke to everyone who came in the church. Scott stood off to the side and observed. So far, so good. No nut cases.

Five minutes before service started, the preacher entered the sanctuary. As he walked down the aisle to the pulpit, Scott gave him some distance. The place was full. The ushers had put chairs at the end of the pews for overflow. This was just the early service. The second one was always bigger.

The first service went off without a problem. Scott escorted the preacher up to his office so he could prepare for the next service. Scott posted the uniformed deputy at the door. He went down to greet his family in the sanctuary.

Bill, Victoria, Sara and the kids were there. Fred surprised everyone by showing up. Maybe Jonas was rubbing off on him.

Scott put his hand to his ear. He heard the deputy say, "Preacher's coming down, going to the back entrance."

"Okay, I'll pick him up at the steps on the second level," Scott answered, speaking into the microphone again.

"I gotta go," he told Sara and rushed off.

Again, the preacher greeted everyone who came through the doors. Once Scott got him to the pulpit, he tried to relax a little. He surely hoped this service went as smoothly as the first one.

As the choir and congregation began to sing "How Great Thou Art," Scott got a call.

"Scott, this is William. I'm in the front vestibule. A strange guy in a tan overcoat just went up to the balcony."

"No problem. I'll check it out," Scott told him.

A strange guy to William could be anybody. William was old school. You dressed up to come to church, no ball caps, tee shirts, or flip flops. Strictly coat and tie.

Scott went through the administrative hallway up to the balcony. He slipped into the back of the balcony just in time to see the man in the tan overcoat sit down. The dark-skinned man sat on the end of the pew about three rows from the glass banister. From the back, the small man had jet black hair with a lot of gel in it. Maybe he was from India. No, Pakistan, he thought. Then it hit him. He was an Arab.

Scott's mind kicked into overdrive. In a split second thoughts raced through: *An Arab. That's interesting. We've had Arabs here before. One spoke in Todd's Sunday school class. Was this the same one? No, this wasn't him. What's he doing now?*

Scott was still standing by the door as the man stood up and looked at his watch.

Where's he going? Scott wondered.

The man exited the pew and Scott saw why he was wearing an overcoat. The barrel of an AK-47 became visible through the front of the coat. The man approached the glass railing and started to pull the weapon out.

Scott observed all this from behind in slow motion. He didn't have time to use his radio. He rushed the Arab man, running full force into him. At first, Scott thought the glass railing would break, but it held. The force of the hit knocked the breath out of the small man. The gunman bent double over the top of the glass. Scott picked up the man's legs and flipped him over. The man landed on his back in the aisle below.

The preacher looked up in disbelief and the whole church fell silent. No one in the congregation, choir and orchestra could believe what they were seeing.

Scott knew the fall wouldn't kill the gunman, but he knew his two hundred pounds coming down on top of him would. The gunman was looking up as he saw Scott vault over the railing. Scott landed feet first on top of the man's chest. All you could hear were breaking ribs and air rushing from the man's lungs. The force of the fall caused Scott's knees to buckle and mash the gunman's upper chest. If he wasn't dead, it wouldn't be long before he was. Then all hell broke loose.

Gunfire erupted from several points around the church. Scott could tell from the sound that all the firing was coming from AK's. Bullets penetrated the wall above his head as he lay on top of the dead gunman.

Scott sprang into action like someone who had been training his whole life for this second. Pulling the rifle from under the gunman, he crouched at the end of a pew, looking for Bill. He moved down the aisle, spotting Bill, Victoria and Sara. Between the rifle fire and screaming he had to get close to Bill to be heard. People were starting to panic and run for exit doors.

"Bill," Scott yelled above the noise, "get everybody down and under a pew." Bill nodded and pushed Victoria down.

"Keep our families safe no matter what," Bill heard him say and he was gone.

The man in front of Bill bent over, then stood up. Bill noticed an ear bud for a radio in his ear. Security team member. Bill saw the man raise a handgun and return fire.

Scott was fighting his way up the aisle. The closer he got to the back of the church, the more the crowd thinned out. Now he could see why. A man wearing a suit and tie had a rifle up to his shoulder, shooting. Scott could tell the man was of Middle Eastern descent and had very little training. The gunman was doing what was called spraying and praying shooting. Not aiming the weapon, just holding it and pulling the trigger. Due to an automatic weapon's tendency to rise, most of the bullets were going over people's heads, although those standing in the choir loft were taking hits.

The gunman was standing next to a pillar holding up the balcony. Scott could see bullets hitting the column. He turned and saw Dwight Justice, one of the security team, shooting from a pew by Bill.

Dwight's last two rounds hit the second gunman in the chest and he went down. The automatic weapon fire continued.

Pushing and pulling people out of his way, Scott made it to the second gunman. The man was still alive. Scott could hear air coming from the wounds in his chest. Scott pulled his pistol from an ankle holster and looked into the man's eyes.

"Why are you doing this," Scott screamed at the injured man.

The gunman looked at Scott and said, "Infidels, we will kill all of you."

Scott stood over the man and pointed his pistol at him and fired.

"You won't be killing anybody."

Dwight saw Scott shoot the man on the floor. He couldn't believe it. Scott's and Dwight's eyes met for a brief moment. Several bullets ripped into Dwight's body and he fell to the floor.

There were at least two more gunmen firing on the congregation. Scott looked around and saw one standing at the rear corner of the large room.

One of the few non-law enforcement members of the security team had produced a weapon and was shooting in the general direction of the third gunman.

The noise and commotion were so great, Scott could not hear Tom's pistol fire. All he could see was the recoil rock back the small pistol in Tom's hand. One round hit its mark in the gunman's left forearm. The 22 round did little damage except to let the gunman know someone was shooting at him. Still firing the rifle, the man pivoted towards Tom. Tom continued squeezing off shots, not realizing his pistol was empty. The rounds from the AK slammed into his body, almost cutting him in half. Scott was yelling for him to get down, but Tom was already dead.

Bill had gotten Victoria and Sara under a pew. Fred grabbed Shay and stuffed her under one. He then lowered his body on top of her. For once in his life he wasn't thinking about sex while on top of a female. Jeff was crawling to the end of the pew when Bill grabbed his arm. "Where do you think you're going?" he yelled as a stream of bullets splintered the wood on the pew in front of him.

"I'm going to help Scott."

Bill could see the young boy was crying. He squirmed from Bill's grip and was gone.

***

In a split second, Scott could see what had to be done. There was no way of reaching the third gunman from where he was. Pushing people out of the way and running over bodies, Scott made his way to the back doors of the sanctuary. One set of doors was clogged with people trying to escape the carnage. At least they were out of the line of fire. The other set of doors was blocked with bodies. Scott turned right, jumped into a pew and ran for the door at the end of it.

The third gunman saw the movement out of the corner of his eye and drew down on Scott. All his rounds hit behind Scott and left a track down the wall. Shooting at a crowd in a spraying motion was much easier than hitting a single moving target. Scott made it to the door and ran out into a large nearly empty hallway.

Scott grabbed his microphone and in a soft, calm voice said, "Security room, we have multiple shooters in the sanctuary. Call 911 now. Request everyone." He didn't know where the next thought came from, but he said it anyway. "There may be a bomb."

Somehow he had to get Sara and the kids out of the building. Scott kept moving. A hand touched Scott's shoulder. He spun around, putting the pistol in the boy's face.

"Dad! Dad, it's only me," Jeff said as the muffled rifle fire continued behind the hall wall. It was one of the few times Jeff had ever called him "Dad" to his face.

Scott didn't give him a chance to speak. "Go back and get everyone out. There may be a bomb somewhere."

"But what…"

"Go now. Get your mom and Shay out," Scott cut him off. Scott had seen this before and shouted, "Now, boy!"

Jeff was startled by Scott's tone and ran off. Scott could only pray.

"Scott, this is Ray Robin. 911 is on their way. You got a shooter in the back right corner and one on the balcony above him. There's another in the prayer garden hallway with a pistol, shooting as he's running.

Scott recognized Ray's voice. Nothing like having a pro in the security room. Scott knew Ray had served in Vietnam and was retired from some local police force. There was no panic in his voice at all.

Scott burst through the door back into the sanctuary. There stood the shooter not five feet away. Scott aimed and fired twice. The man's head exploded. Scott had always been advised that his .380 was too small for the job. Not at this range and not this time.

"Scott, the next shooter is directly above you at the glass railing."

Scott grabbed the AK on the floor, checked the magazine, cleared the last round and put the stock to his shoulder. Stepping out from beneath the balcony, he began to fire. Glass, wood and then blood began to rain down on him. Scott continued shooting as the man fell. The gunman just missed falling onto Scott, who kept firing as the man lay on the floor in front of him.

Finally an older man put his hand on Scott's forearm and pushed down. "I think he's dead, son." Scott looked into the old man's eyes. He had seen him around the church, but never given him much thought. Somehow, by either his touch or through his eyes the man conveyed to Scott the pain and outrage of the whole affair.

"Scott, the last shooter is heading for the prayer garden exit." The voice in Scott's ear bud brought him back to the reality of the situation. "He's in a hurry to get out."

Scott didn't need an explanation of why. All he could think of was "bomb." The prayer garden door was just steps away outside the sanctuary. Scott stood for a moment to observe the carnage. Except for some groans and sobbing the sanctuary was quiet.

The old man holding Scott's arm urged, "You'd better go, boy. Finish it."

Fate, faith and the human mind are all strange things. Fate put Scott, Bill and others together that morning. Faith would bring them through, but it would be the human mind that would suffer the most.

Pastor Carol preached that God's hand was in everything. As Scott rushed towards the exit, he wondered where it was this morning. God's hand had swept the sanctuary. Yes, there were dead and dying people all over the church. Where was God's hand now? Had he let only the sinful get shot? If so, why wasn't everyone dead? They all would be if Scott didn't find the bomb. And where did that thought come from? If it hadn't been for Scott and his security team would there have been a greater number killed? Was that God's work? Doctors and EMS personnel belonging to the church were already working as sirens could be heard in the distance.

Bill lifted his head above the pew once the gunfire had stopped. He saw Scott and an older man talking in the far corner. Victoria was weeping, still under the pew. Bill touched her shaking body. "It's over. You can come out now."

Sara stood up. "Jeff! Jeff!" she yelled. He wasn't in sight. She turned to the pulpit. Some parishioners were already gathering and kneeling, silently praying.

"Mom! Mom, help me!"

Sara heard Shay's voice and began looking on the floor and under the pews for her.

"Mom, are you okay?"

"Yes! Yes, where are you?" and Sara began to weep.

"Tell Fred to get off me."

Sara spotted Fred's dark hair, his back covered in blood.

"Bill, help me!"

Bill and Sara both pulled at Fred. With great effort they were able to pull him from under the pew. His back was riddled with bullet holes and wood splinters from the pews.

"Shay, baby, are you hurt?" Sara asked as Shay scrambled from beneath the pew.

"No. No, I don't think so." She was covered with Fred's blood.

"Where's Scott?" Sara asked Bill.

"I don't know. He was over there a second ago." Bill pointed to the far corner.

"Mom, we've got to get out of here. Dad said there may be a bomb," Jeff told her as he came through the door closest to them. She was so overwhelmed to see him the words did not register, but Bill understood.

"Jeff, get your mom, Shay and Victoria outside any way you can. I'll get the rest of the people moving," Bill said as he headed to the pulpit. Bill went to the podium. There sitting behind it was the pastor, a bullet hole in his left shoulder. It was a painful wound, but not life-threatening. Bill explained in the fewest words possible what was happening and what needed to be done. Bill helped the preacher to his feet.

Bill said in a loud voice and flat tone, "Everybody, we need to clear the building. Help anyone you can and move outside as fast as possible."

The preacher got down on his knees and began to pray. Bill couldn't believe his eyes. No one moved. Everyone continued praying as before. Bill watched as more people made their way to the pulpit. By the door he saw Victoria, Sara, Shay and Jeff praying. He sank to his knees alongside the preacher. The preacher put his arm around Bill and said, "It'll be all right, brother," and they both began to pray.

Scott was far from praying. Once out the sanctuary door, he began looking for the shooter. The voice in his ear bud told him where and what to look for.

"He's right in front of you."

Scott spotted him. He was right behind him. The last terrorist still had a handgun in his hand hanging at his side. In his other hand, the man fumbled with a cell phone. Scott knew he couldn't let him dial that phone. He ran as hard as he could at the man's back. With the force of a truck, Scott pushed the man into the center post dividing the double doors.

They hit the post with such force that it dislodged and both men fell to the ground. People coming out of the church were in such shock they just moved out of the way and kept on walking. The force and surprise of the hit caused the gunman to drop both his phone and pistol. Scott was able to keep his wits about him, but the other fellow was stunned from the impact. Scott got up first and picked up the phone and the weapon. He grabbed the shooter by his hair and dragged him to the side of the building, out of the way of the dazed people.

"Where is the bomb?" Scott asked calmly.

"What are you talking about? I'm a church member."

The report from the pistol was louder than Scott expected, but not as loud as the man's scream. Scott looked at the weapon, a Glock 9mm. Nice piece. When the noise from the blast had dissipated in his ears he could hear the man's screams. Scott had shot him in the knee.

"Let me ask you again. Where is the bomb?"

"There is no bomb. We were just supposed to shoot as many as we could."

Bang! This time it was the left elbow.

"That was my last question. You've got six or seven major joints left. Stop me at any time."

Bang! The other knee was gone.

"This isn't the way Americans are supposed to be!" the man cried out.

Scott had used the last round. The Glock was empty. He threw it aside. Pulling out his nine millimeter from the small of his back, he pointed it at the man's ankle.

"Ok, stop! Please stop! There is a suitcase under the staircase to the balcony. It's blue with red stripes and…"

The man's voice trailed off as Scott sprinted back into the church. With the shooting stopped, people had stopped the mad panic. Most were walking around in a fog. The front hall was so packed with people he had no hope of getting through. Scott entered the sanctuary.

It was quiet except for the moaning of the injured. There were bodies bent over pews and laying in the aisles. At one set of double doors was a pile of people all shot in the back while trying to escape the massacre.

Scott moved through a pew as opposed to going around to the other aisle. He could see hundreds of people praying at the altar. Next to the podium, he saw Preacher Carol on his knees, blood on his shoulder. Next to him was Bill.

"Bill!" he shouted. "Bill!" louder this time.

Bill looked up and Scott waved to him, motioning for him to come. "Preacher, I need to go."

Carol didn't say anything, just nodded and continued leading the prayer.

As Bill moved towards Scott, he took in the view of the whole sanctuary. It was a mess, but considering the number of rounds expended, it should have been worse. As Bill approached, Scott informed him of the bomb.

"There's a bomb under the steps. I'm going to need some help. Meet me at the front steps. We're going to need a car or golf cart."

Bill was gone in a flash. He understood Scott's plan without explanation. Get the device as far away as possible.

Scott opened the small door to the storage area under the steps. His right hand searched for a light switch. Having only been in here once or twice before, Scott didn't have any idea where the light was. He couldn't find a switch. He held his hand out in front of him and felt a string. Pulling it a small, single, overhead bulb came on.

Sitting in the middle of the floor surrounded by things somebody thought needed to be saved was the suitcase.

Scott grabbed the handle. What if this thing is rigged to go off when you move it? Nobody lives forever. He jerked up the bag and started for the front door.

The front doors were open and a few people were heading for them when the SWAT team streamed through them, swinging their weapons from side to side and shouting for everyone to get down. The parishioners were numb. Some fell to the floor; others kept on walking. The officers continued to yell, but not many people responded.

One deputy put his gun to Scott's head. "Freeze," he screamed, "or I'll shoot."

How ironic to have survived a massacre only to be shot by the good guys.

"Hold on, I know this man," said another deputy as he removed his goggles.

Scott recognized the deputy but couldn't think of his name.

"What happened here? What's in the case?"

"I don't have time for this." Scott shoved the case towards the two deputies. "It's full of explosives. You want it?"

The two deputies looked at the case, then each other. They don't let dummies on the SWAT team and both shook their heads no. They cleared a path to let Scott exit the building. Coming through the doors, Scott saw Bill sitting in a cart waiting for him.

"You took long enough," Bill said.

"I got held up." Scott put the case on the cart and started to get on.

"No way, friend. You've done enough. Why risk it?" and Bill was off.

Scott almost fell on the ground, regained his balance and started after the cart as it sped away. Bill looked back, knowing Scott couldn't catch him and smiled.

Scott stood next to the deputy who had recognized him. Adam. His first name was Adam, Scott remembered.

"It's a good thing you knew me. I believe that boy would have shot me." Both men agreed. They stood watching the golf cart as it sped through the parking lot.

"Come on, Bill. Leave it. That's far enough," Scott said in a whisper.

"No, it's not, from the size of the case," Adam said.

Several EMT's emerged from the church with injured men and women. They were being laid on the front lawn, dead and dying to the left and treatable wounds to the right. There was already a line of bodies under white sheets. Some of the men had their suit jackets pulled over their heads.

"Damn," Scott said as he bolted off with Adam in tow.

"What's the matter?"

"I left one alive, but I can't find his cell phone. I must have dropped it. I think that was how he planned to set off the bomb.

As the two men rounded the corner, Scott was surprised to see the man trying to crawl through the grass. There was the cell phone a few feet from the wounded terrorist. Scott drew his pistol to shoot.

"No!" Adam yelled and jumped for the phone. Adam was stretched out like a baseball player stealing home. The shot up man made one final, feeble lunge, but Adam's hands pushed the phone out of reach as he slid on the grass. The terrorist began shouting at them in Arabic.

Adam grabbed the phone and rolled over on his back, holding the phone up like a prize. A swarm of officers surrounded Scott, yelling for him to drop the gun. Scott was in a shooting stance and let the pistol fall while keeping his arms outstretched.

The cops converged on him. Scott was amazed at how fast they had cuffed him and stood him back on his feet, the whole time yelling at him. At least they learned something with all that training, Scott thought.

Then the ground shook at the explosion of 60 pounds of plastic explosives. The noise was deafening. The concussion knocked people off their feet. Scott wondered if Bill made it and collapsed on the ground.

27

No trace of Bill's body was found and from the size of the crater it was no wonder. The fifth gunman revealed that several more churches and synagogues were targeted. Christians, Jews and Muslims came together to protect each other's places of worship.

Most of the security team had been shot at the start of the melee. The gunman told an interrogator that he had visited the church several times to take notes. The police found more guns and bomb-making material in a rented mobile home. There were many arrests and seizures.

**

Victoria was devastated over Bill's death, but her convictions and belief in God helped her cope. Sara and Shay were shaken up, but in good spirits. They provided Victoria with support. Jeff had a bullet wound in the leg that would heal. Scott was okay. He went on as if the church shooting was an everyday thing. The police and FBI questioned him about the shooters he had killed. The one that bothered them the most was the shooter Scott threw from the balcony. Why was there a single bullet to his head? They didn't like Scott's answer.

"I guess you just had to be there."

"Why didn't you kill the one who told you where the bomb was?" asked FBI Agent Bishop.

"I left him alive in case the bomb wasn't where he said it was. I was going back to finish him off when the SWAT guys jumped me and put me in cuffs. Why didn't you finish him off?" Scott asked.

Bishop looked at the two way mirror in the room and said, "That's not what we do."

The agents behind the glass looked at each other.

"Man, I'm glad he's on our side."

"I'd say, he killed three bad guys and did you see the fourth? He'll never walk without a walker and that one arm is useless."

"We need to hire him," one agent said as they all left the small room.

Agent Bishop had one last question for Scott but didn't want anyone else to hear it.

"Were you and Bill August friends?"

"Yes, he was my friend," Scott said proudly.

"Do you have any idea where he got his money from?"

Scott thought that was a strange question but answered it anyway.

"He told me it was an inheritance."

Bishop looked long and hard at Scott. No, he wasn't lying and Bishop wasn't going to open a can of worms.

The three men Bishop had arrested didn't know where the money from the truck was. The agent had found Bill's other U.S. accounts, even the ones under a false name. Where Bill had come up with another Social Security Number was anybody's guess. Bishop knew about all the trips to the Caymans, but he couldn't access the accounts there.

Bishop wasn't stupid. He knew Bill had something to do with the missing money. Bill was a hero for what he had done and Bishop wasn't about to tarnish the image. The country needed more like him. Scott, on the other hand, was a different story altogether. He bore watching.

28

Several weeks later, Victoria announced she was pregnant. God surely worked in mysterious ways. Scott and Sara saw Victoria off at the airport. They told her not to worry about the house. They would look after it. Victoria told Scott to use it whenever he wanted.

"It'll make a great getaway for you and Sara."

Before parting, Victoria handed Scott an envelope. "What's this?"

"Bill would have wanted you to have this. Don't open it 'till I'm in the air."

Victoria and Sara embraced.

"Please come see me as soon as you can." Victoria left.

***

The church had a service for the slain. No media of any kind was allowed in the building. There was a large police presence. Scott and his new team were patrolling as before. Everyone involved with the investigation respected Scott's wish and didn't release his name. When church members were asked who the biggest savior that Easter morning was, they all answered, "God."

***

Victoria went straight to the condo. The front door was unlocked and she went in. It was empty and quiet. She ran out the back sliding doors to the beach. She looked up the beach towards Georgetown.

There by the clear water, looking out to sea stood a man. He turned and waved to her. She couldn't contain herself and sprinted to him.

"Bill, I missed you so much! I hated having to act like you were gone."

"Sorry, Vic. It had to be this way."

"But why?" she asked.

Bill wanted to come clean, tell her everything, but he wasn't ready yet. He knew he couldn't go on with this charade and he wouldn't. The explosion was perfect for him to fade away.

While Special Agent Bishop was sorting through the mess at the church, Bill made his way to the coast.

He had chartered a sailboat to take him to the Grand Caymans. Now he felt displaced, like he was homeless, more like countryless. He would have to fix things and make them right again, but how?

He spied a man standing on the balcony of his condo. By the time Vic turned to see what Bill was looking at, he was gone.

"What?" she asked.

"Nothing, I was just… It's just… I thought I saw something. Wait here a minute," he told her. "I'll get us a couple of cold drinks. When I get back, I'll tell you why," and he was off to the condo. Bill climbed the steps to the balcony two at a time and went in.

"Hello, Special Agent Bishop, what brings you to the Caymans?"

Acknowledgements

First, to my family, who thought they would never see any of my work in print.

To Robert Hefner, for proof-reading and being honest.

To Jean Hefner, for helping me with the cover and being brutally honest with her editing.

And last, but not least, Don Rabon, for nudging, pushing and prying me along.

If I forgot anybody, too bad, but you know who you are.

COMING SOON "THE RESTORATION"
(A sequel to "The Inheritance)

CPSIA information can be obtained
at www.ICGtesting.com
Printed in the USA
FFOW03n1439220915
17054FF

9 781943 842568